THE BOOK OF KENYA

THE BOOK OF
KENYA

Gerald Cubitt
PHOTOGRAPHS

Eric Robins
TEXT

COLLINS and HARVILL PRESS
London, 1980

Frontispiece: View of the Rift Valley from the Tot escarpment

Colour transparencies taken on
Agfachrome 5oS film and processed by the
Agfa reversal station in Nairobi, Kenya.

© 1980 Gerald Cubitt Photographs
© 1980 Eric Robins Text
ISBN 0 00 216044-7
Maps by Tom Stalker-Miller
Made and printed in Great Britain
by W. S. Cowell Ltd, Ispwich
for Collins, St James's Place and
Harvill Press, 30A Pavilion Road, London, SW1

CONTENTS

AUTHOR'S NOTE

This book reflects in many aspects my long and happy associations with Kenya.

Writing it, therefore, was a pleasant task, made even more rewarding by the friendly, and valuable assistance given to me in my researches by Jan Hemsing, Marion Kaplan, Avice Rapley, Jimmy Smart, Ilge Koplimae, Jim Allen, officials of the Kenya Railways, and the Chief Librarian and staff of the MacMillan Library, Nairobi.

My sincere thanks to them, and to all who made any contribution to this work.

ERIC ROBINS
Nairobi, 1979

TO JANET

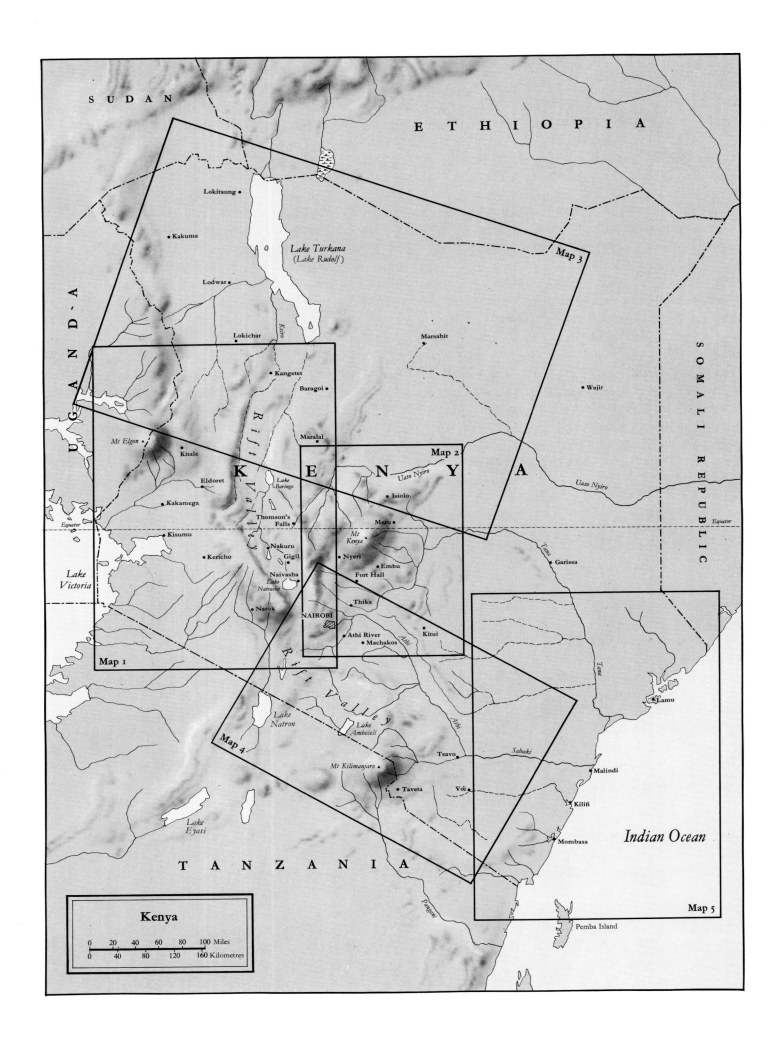

SUDAN

ETHIOPIA

U G A N D A

SOMALI REPUBLIC

Lokitaung •

Kakuma •

Lake Turkana
(Lake Rudolf)

Map 3

Lodwar •

Kerio

Marsabit •

Lokichar •

Wajir •

Kangetet •

Baragoi •

Maralal •

Map 2

Rift Valley

Mt Elgon ▲

Kitale •

K E N Y A

Uaso Nyiro

Eldoret •

Isiolo •

Uaso Nyiro

Kakamega •

Lake
Baringo

Thomson's
Falls •

Meru •

Equator

Equator

Kisumu •

Nakuru •

*Mt
Kenya* ▲

Garissa •

Kericho •

Gigil •

Nyeri •

Tana

Athi

Lake
Victoria

Naivasha •

Lake
Naivasha

Embu •

Fort Hall •

Thika •

Narok •

NAIROBI

Athi River •

Kitui •

Athi

Machakos •

Rift

Lamu •

Map 1

Lake
Natron

Valley

Lake
Amboseli

Sabaki

Malindi •

Map 4

Athi

Tsavo •

Mt Kilimanjaro ▲

Voi •

Kilifi •

Taveta •

Lake
Eyasi

Mombasa •

Indian Ocean

T A N Z A N I A

Pangati

Map 5

Pemba Island

Kenya

0   20   40   60   80   100 Miles

0   40   80   120   160 Kilometres

I

African Eden

'I speak of Africa and golden joys'
— William Shakespeare, Henry IV, Pt. 2

Variety — in her people, climate and terrain — is the invigorating spice of life in Kenya.

Within the country's 225,000 square miles, Kenya embraces steamy rain forests and sun-scorched plains, snow-capped peaks and parched deserts, rainbow reefs and tumbling trout streams, bamboo jungles and bustling mini-cities teeming with overloaded buses, asthmatic lorries, hand-carts piled high with pineapples, battered jalopies and ruby-red Mercedes.

While the goatherds' wells run dry in a drought-stricken corner of the land, less than a hundred miles away a tea or coffee-growing region will record two or three inches of rain in a single night's blustering storm.

When the wheat-growing highlands are shrouded in mist or the evening chill on the Equator is below zero, the coastal sunshine and humidity create a monumental thirst that only a frosty glass of iced, fresh lime juice can slake.

The 16,000,000 Africans who make up the bulk of Kenya's multiracial population belong to four main ethnic groups, and these in turn divide into some fifty tribes or sub-tribes speaking a dozen different tongues.

Although small-scale farming, animal husbandry and sea or lake fishing are the traditional occupations of most of the various tribal groups, over the past two or three decades Africans have successfully entered a number of the professions and occupations typical of contemporary Kenyan society.

There are bewigged Kikuyu barristers and white-coated hospital doctors and dentists; Samburu company directors; Kamba engineers and architects; Maasai cabinet ministers; senior civil servants from the Luo people, as well as men and women public relations officers, newspaper and magazine editors, stockbrokers, business executives, book-keepers, pyrethrum planters, managers of game lodges, and shopkeepers from all tribes.

People living in Kenya who belong to a variety of linguistic and religious groups originating in India and Pakistan are classified as 'Asians'. In the past, they supplied most of Kenya's trading, artisan and clerical classes and, although Africans continue to make rapid progress in these fields, these descendants of Indian labourers still occupy an important part in the country's commercial and industrial life.

Many British farmers who formed the basis of the colonial white community before Kenyan independence have sold their lands to the government for African settlement and gone back with their families to Kensington, Winchester or Harrogate. Others have stayed on as safari operators, businessmen or ranch managers. In addition to these expatriates, the post-independence ranks of the Europeans are being substantially increased by new faces in the private sector and by advisers and technicians joining the government services and the various UN and foreign aid missions based in Kenya.

Tourists come to Kenya in increasing numbers every year from France, Holland, Italy, Scandinavia, Switzerland, Britain, Germany, America, Canada, Japan, and several other countries. For all of them, Kenya with its natural charm, polyglot colour and primeval thrills of the world's last vast open zoo, is 'The Land of Discovery'.

Some citizens, and visitors alike, parody Mark Twain and insist that 'when God made Heaven he copied Kenya'.

Kenya's first settler— Early Man— wandered out of the mists of antiquity to the volcano-studded shores of the windswept 'Jade Sea', now known as Lake Turkana. There he left his bones and those of the animals he hunted for palaeontologists to find some two million years later. He also scattered his crude stone tools over his camp sites, and these have survived in many places where his bones have perished.

This must have been a cradle of mankind, the Garden of Eden — the astonishingly early dates obtained by scientists for these sites leave little doubt about man's East African origins.

For hundreds of thousands of years Stone Age man hunted in his paradise beside the Rift Valley lakes, slowly perfecting his weapons and techniques. He had to contend with ancestral elephants bigger than those of today, pigs the size of rhino, and formidable great baboons which he slaughtered in large numbers for food, and for which he had to compete with fierce carnivores.

Eventually he learnt to make bows and arrows, grindstones and pottery. Then Kushitic pastoralists came down from the north, bringing their herds of goats and cattle. Others arrived from the west with a knowledge of iron-working and agriculture. These were probably speakers of the Bantu languages, who established themselves in the west and the east of the country, leaving the central highlands to the pastoralists.

The earliest written record— Kenya's first tourist guide book— dates from around the time of the introduction of iron-working. Known as the *Periplus of the Erythrean Sea*, it was a pilot's account of trading voyages in the Indian Ocean, written by an unknown Greek from Alexandria about AD 120.

He tells of his visit to some palmy islands that were almost certainly the Lamu group, and of a large island further south that is now Mombasa, Kenya's main port and second city. The author describes how some traders from southern Arabia had already settled on the coast of East Africa and married natives, although most of them sailed home again after obtaining their cargoes of ivory, rhino horn and turtle-shell.

The north-east monsoon, which blows from November to March, brought the Arab dhows with their lateen sails and high, ornamented poops to the land of Sinj — blacks — as they called it (the Greeks knew it as Azania, 'the dry country'). After a few months' trading, they returned with the south-west monsoon from May to September.

The handsome wooden craft were manned by swarthy turbanned seamen, brothers of Sinbad: some of his *Arabian Nights* tales have, in fact, the old Kenya coast as their setting.

One story, featuring a strange island, is believed to have its origins and inspiration in manta rays weighing half-a-ton that explode from the sea and blot out the sun as they sail over the heads of African fishermen crouched in fear in their dug-out canoes; the rays hit the sea again with a roar like a booming cannon.

'The captain came close to the shore, and many of us left the ship and landed. Some made fires and some cooked food. Some went to swim in the sea, and to wash their clothes. There was much eating and drinking and playing and sleeping. Now as I was walking I heard the voice of the captain call out to us: "Ho there! Run, all of you . . . God help us, for this island on which you stand is no true island, quiet in the middle of the sea . . . When you lit your fires on it, it moved. Indeed, it is nothing else but a great fish." Suddenly the island shook under my feet, and then it sank into the sea with all that was on it, and the water rushed over us in great waves. With the others I went down, down, down into the deep, but God saved me from death.'

The dhows' cargoes of oriental carpets, gem-encrusted bracelets, carved chests, dates and spices, bartered for ivory, copra, grain and charcoal, have barely changed over the ages.

The stately deep-sea vessels still drop anchor in Mombasa's old port early each year, and their crews take their orders in Kiswahili, the venerable language of the coast.

After the *Periplus* came a 'dark age' lasting about eight hundred years, with only Ptolemy's *Geography* to throw a faint but tantalising glimmer of light. He told of a towering dome covered in snow which must have been Kilimanjaro, Africa's highest and most noble mountain which stands at 19,342 feet, and of great inland lakes and the 'Mountains of the Moon' (Ruwenzori). No European was to sight any of them for another fifteen hundred years.

The oldest known Islamic settlement in East Africa is on Manda, one of the Lamu islands, dating from about AD 900. During the next few centuries wealthy Persian and Arab merchants set up rival trading colonies on the Lamu islands, at Malindi and its satellite town of Gedi, and at Mombasa.

They built solid houses of stone or coral and lime and surrounded themselves with luxurious silks, porcelain and silver. These zealous Moslems also built mosques, many of which survive, and made converts among the Africans. Intermarriage with the local people gave rise to a new tribe, the Swahili, with its distinctive language and culture.

The coast was East Africa's 'window on the world', but the Arabs and Swahili neither knew nor cared what went on in the interior so long as they got their ivory. It was brought to them by long lines of sweating tribesmen for the meagre reward of beads and lengths of cloth. Slavery was a secondary consideration until the 19th century.

Shards of delicate Chinese porcelain can still be picked up along the silvery shores of Kenya. It was imported via India, although in 1415 Malindi traders thought it worth making direct contact with the Emperor of China by shipping him a giraffe as a gift.

Beautiful Chinese bowls were inset in the walls of mosques, for example at Gedi. The dank, haunted ruins there were all but swallowed up by tangled jungle until cleared during ten years of arduous excavation. The town, covering 45 acres, lay concealed in this eerie forest since the 16th century when it was suddenly abandoned by its 2,500 citizens. Nobody knows why, though there are theories that the water supplies dried up, or that it was sacked by tribesmen. It remains a ghost town, inhabited only by spitting cobras, monkeys and the rare golden-rumped elephant shrew.

Before Gedi became an African Angkor Wat, the Portuguese sailed to Kenya seeking a route to the fabled riches of the East. In the vanguard of the galleons was the flagship of the cruel but courageous Vasco da Gama who flew the emblem of the Order of Christ, a blood-red cross on a white background. On Easter Sunday 1498 he tacked his caravel over the reefs into Malindi Bay and went ashore to sign an alliance with its sultan. Outside the ruler's palace the explorer set up a stone cross as a symbol of his hasty friendship of convenience; it still stands on a headland overlooking a turquoise sea.

As Vasco da Gama sailed away to discover India, other rulers along the Kenya coast, less submissive than the sultan of Malindi, were ruthlessly conquered by Portuguese naval and military might. Mombasa, an important port of call on the trade route to India, was put to the sword three times before its sultan and his army were finally crushed in 1505 by 1,500 men and an armada of 23 ships. The Arabs' bloody revenge was to come many years later.

Meanwhile the Mombasans were offered help from a surprising source in the form of hordes of cannibals. Originating in Zaire, the Zimba had swept up the coast from the south consuming all in their path like a swarm of locusts. Far from helping, they massacred and ate most of the inhabitants of Mombasa, only to be defeated themselves at Malindi, Mombasa's rival and Portugal's ally.

This was only the beginning of Mombasa's troubles; soon after, the town was threatened by shiploads of fierce Turkish pirates. In 1593 the Portuguese built a thick-walled fort which they hoped would prove impregnable. They called it Fort Jesus and sited it on a high ridge of coral overlooking the Indian Ocean at a point where ships were forced close to shore by channel currents and shoals.

The coral bank was hacked back to provide a vertical face below the fort's stout walls, each covered by a protective bastion. Cannon platforms gave wide fields of fire.

Although the main masonry was built within two years, construction of Fort Jesus, section by section, went on for some time.

There the Portuguese installed Vasco da Gama's old ally, the sultan of Malindi, as the puppet overlord of Mombasa. But the sultan eventually fell out with his hosts and escaped to the interior in fear of his life. The man's flight was of no avail for the Portuguese paid a band of Nyika tribesmen a sackful of maize — one of the commodities they had imported into East Africa from South America — to track down and murder the fugitive.

Portuguese rule became increasingly challenged, and a new power, the Omanis, arose to 'free the people from the iron yoke'.

In 1696 the Imam of Oman sent a large fleet and 3,000 soldiers to destroy Fort Jesus, cornerstone of the Portuguese grip on East Africa. Some 2,500 people were crammed into the fort to defend it as the Omani ships appeared on the horizon.

The 33-months' siege and defence of the fort was a grisly epic, claiming the lives of 800 Portuguese and their 3,000 Swahili followers.

Within a year the defenders were reduced by constant assaults from Arab hordes, starvation, bubonic plague and other diseases into a gallant group consisting of the commander, two soldiers, a priest and seventy black followers, including forty women who fought as bravely as the men. The fort commandant, the priest and soldiers died before a small relief force arrived in 1698.

The Portuguese and their primitive troops fought on against renewed assaults. When at last the howling Omanis poured over the walls from scaling ladders with flashing scimitars, the garrison strength had shrunk to eight Portuguese, three Indians and two African women. The new commander was cut down as he rushed into a band of attacking Arabs, firing his musket. Two wounded Portuguese soldiers led a crowd of the enemy into the gunpower room of Fort Jesus on the pretext that it contained a hoard of gold — then, with themselves inside, lit a wax taper and blew it up.

So ended their country's rule in Kenya; and from then on the Portuguese were driven out of their coastal strongholds one by one.

Contact between the hinterland and the coast slowly increased through the Arab caravans of slaves and ivory-carriers. Sadly, the cruel slave trade had been started by the Africans themselves. Martial tribes who preyed on weaker neighbours sold their captives to the Arabs in exchange for weapons that enabled them to wage more effective wars to obtain even more slaves. The Arabs in turn sold the hapless slaves to the owners of tea, coffee, sugar and tobacco plantations around the world.

Kenya got off relatively lightly owing to the formidable presence of the Maasai, who often did not allow caravans to cross their country. The worst of the trade took place further south, in what is now Tanzania, with the main slave market in Zanzibar. Nevertheless a number of slave trails across Kenya ended at Lamu. Month after month there arrived in the town square the pitiful survivors of cross-country marches of hundreds of miles — men, women and children, yoked and manacled to each other, whose emaciated bodies bore the scars of fearful lashings by brutal overseers and whose sunken eyes told of starvation, exhaustion and despair.

It has been calculated that by the time slavery was abolished some ten million people had been captured and sold in the open markets of East Africa.

In the 19th century Britain took part in 'the scramble for Africa' with the greatest reluctance, and for humanitarian rather than acquisitive reasons. She had no wish to add great expanses of barbarous territory to her burdens, but she was determined to do away with the slave trade, which had been outlawed in her own overseas possessions early in the century.

Her other obsession was to discover the source of the Nile, but just as the slave traders had been daunted by the Maasai in Kenya so too were the explorers. All expeditions set forth for the great lakes well to the south, through Tanzania. The first Europeans to take a pioneering interest in the interior of Kenya, in fact, were not explorers at all, but missionaries.

Dr Johann Ludwig Krapf, a German who joined the Church Missionary Society in England, founded a mission station at Rabai near Mombasa in 1844. There he was joined by Dr Johann Rebmann, who had sighted Kilimanjaro. A year later, in 1849, Dr Krapf saw from afar the twin peaks of Kere Nyaga, the Kikuyu name for 'mountains of whiteness' and mythical home in the clouds of their god Ngai. A contraction of this name, Kenya, has been bestowed on the country as well as the mountain.

Geographers in Europe scoffed at Dr Krapf's claim that he had found a mountain with 'two large horns or pillars covered with a white substance' which he surmised was snow. The armchair scientists — wrong again — regarded snow on the Equator as a contradiction in terms.

Then, in 1883, a Scottish explorer, Joseph Thomson, made his epic journey through Maasailand and confirmed the existence of the snow-capped mountain. More important, he proved that it was possible to reach Lake Victoria through the country of the dreaded Maasai warriors.

Determined to oppose the slave trade, Britain established her 'sphere of influence' over the northern part of East Africa (Kenya) and left the rest (Tanzania) to the Germans. She was even more interested in Uganda in order to keep control of the Upper Nile and hence Egypt.

To a certain extent unruly tribes were 'pacified' through the medium of an imperial trading company which, by 1888, had established a chain of mud-walled forts across Kenya. Six years later a Protectorate over Uganda was established, and in 1895 a reluctant Foreign Office took over the administration of Kenya, which was known as the British East Africa Protectorate.

The stumbling block to the development of the country was the total lack of communications. The trading company had never made a profit, but obviously the potential was there. Britain therefore, again after great parliamentary reluctance, made a momentous decision which turned the course of Kenyan history. She decided to build a railway from Mombasa to a port on the inland sea of Lake Victoria.

It was a monumental and heroic enterprise.

The railway meandered across the landscape, skirting hills and mountains, and the Africans with their aptitude for a simple, vivid phrase, called it 'The Iron Snake'.

Hostile natives, wild animals and tropical diseases took heavy toll of the engineers and their construction teams of coolies brought over from India for the project.

In the Tsavo area of Kenya, about a hundred miles inland, two man-eating lions stalked and killed more than a hundred Indian and African workers in the course of a few months. The man-eaters maintained a reign of terror on the line until they were cornered and shot by J. H. Patterson, the chief engineer.

Later, as the line progressed, a white railways superintendent was seized in the sleeping compartment of his stationary coach by another lion and carried off to a horrible death.

Before the railway was completed, disease and accidents had claimed 2,493 of the 32,000 imported Indian labourers, while casualties among the Africans who went ahead of the construction teams clearing the bush were uncounted.

On Kenya's highlands, 326 miles from the sea and close to an old slave route, a small party of British army engineers led by Sgt. George Ellis from Surrey put up a survey camp of green canvas tents. The site they chose was a papyrus swamp of black-cotton soil where, not surprisingly, there had never been any human habitation. But there were lions, rhino, leopards and deadly snakes in plenty, and at night a chorus of thousands of bullfrogs provided a maddening cacophony for the intrepid Sgt. Ellis and his men.

The statuesque Maasai nomads who watered their cattle at this inhospitable spot called it Uaso Nyarobe ('cold water') after the narrow river fed by a mountain stream that ran through it.

The 'Iron Snake' reached this bleak location — Nairobi — on May 30, 1899, six days after Queen Victoria's birthday and as one of Sgt. Ellis' soldiers was snatched from his tent by a black-maned lion and devoured.

Nairobi, situated at 5,235 feet, became a muddy shantytown (although in the dry season it lay under a pall of red dust) filled with swashbuckling pioneers, Indian traders and lumbering ox-wagons. It was all reminiscent of the American West.

Government Road,
Nairobi, in the 1920s

The railway had cost five million pounds and the British Government was anxious to encourage settlers to develop the country and offset this expenditure. At first the response was not encouraging, though some of the Indians who had helped to build the railroad decided to stay and others from their homeland followed. They were the forerunners of Kenya's *duka wallahs*, small traders who presided over ramshackle stores throughout the country and sold almost anything to anybody, from a reel of cotton to a hurricane lamp.

In the year that the railway reached Nairobi, down the quagmire of its main — and only — street rode a long-haired hunter-explorer who, when he had entered the country from the deserts of the north two years earlier, had recognised it as a land of opportunity. He had decided then and there to abandon his estates in England and make his home in Kenya.

Lord Delamere, the third baron of this name, was a fiery, roistering aristocrat, the first of many colourful characters to put down their roots in Kenya. Not long after there followed a wild bunch of white settlers from Australia, South Africa, Britain, Canada, New Zealand, Greece, Scandinavia and Italy.

Although superficially a playboy of the age (whose weekend sport was shooting out the gas mantles of Nairobi's street lamps with his revolver from a careering bullock cart as he brandished his wide-brimmed hat), Lord Delamere had his serious and steely side. He saw the picturesque aspects of Kenya and the potentialities for gentlemen farmers with grit and a spirit of adventure — the sun-dappled streams, misty mountain ranges, noble forests, golden plains, flowering trees, and sweeping parklands that recalled rural England.

Never a man to take 'No' for an answer, the bold baron won over the British Government to his view after the administration of the Protectorate had been switched to the Colonial Office in 1903.

On the way to Lord Delamere's goal, there had been only one, slightly daunting, hurdle.

Whitehall had flirted with the notion of making *his* 'White Highlands' north of Nairobi an embryo Zionist state.

The British settlers dealt with this threat in typical *macho* fashion. When a party of Jewish elders came to view the Promised Land, Delamere's horsemen sited their camp in the path of a herd of elephants, which scared away the visitors for good.

So the colonials were left in peace to develop their cattle and sheep ranches,

17

their maizelands, coffee plantations and billowing wheat fields . . . left in peace to live it up in Nairobi every so often away from the rigours and cares of the land.

The most popular 'watering hole' in Nairobi, among the blueblooded ranchers (who shot big game from its upper windows), was the Norfolk Hotel. It had been opened in 1904 as 'Civilization in the Bush', with a French chef and a manager who could speak 'most' European languages. Lord Delamere's hooded rickshaw still stands on the terrace of this mock-Tudor monument to Edwardian nostalgia.

Tribesmen with spears and poisoned arrows wandered freely, and pig-tailed Maasai warriors smeared with mud and red ochre killed lions single-handed, where busy streets and tall buildings today constitute the modern capital city of Nairobi — the 'Crossroads of Africa'.

The Norfolk was then the natural meeting place of the ebullient farmer-settlers (who blamed their crazy antics on the altitude), big game hunters fresh from the trail in ten-gallon hats with leopard-skin bands, remittance men, confidence tricksters, and general riff-raff washed up on the 'Dark Continent'. They delighted in quick-draw matches to shoot bottles of whisky and gin off the shelves of the Norfolk's crowded bar. Afterwards there would be a whip-round amid the debris to pay for the damage and placate the terrified barman.

For all the rowdyism, the Norfolk was known as the 'House of Lords' on account of the preponderance of aristocrats in the hotel's guest register, including the Earl of Warwick and Lords Cardross and Cranworth.

On his retirement as the 26th President of the United States, Theodore ('Teddy') Roosevelt set out from the Norfolk on a hunting trip that broke all records for size and splendour. Five hundred African porters, each carrying a 60 lb. headload of rifles, ammunition boxes, tents, canvas baths, stores and other equipment, accompanied the bandoliered ex-president and his son, Kermit, on this unique luxury safari, the highlight of which was lion-spearing on foot. Roosevelt was as happy an extrovert as any man in his hunting entourage.

He wrote on his way back to America:

'There are no words that can tell the hidden spirit of the wilderness; that can reveal its mystery, its melancholy and its charm.

'There is delight in the hardy life of the open . . . in the thrill of the fight with dangerous game.

'Apart from this, yet mingled with it, is the strong attraction of the silent places, of large tropic moons, and the splendour of the new stars; where the wanderer sees the awful glory of the sunrise and sunset in the wide spaces of the earth, unworn of Man, and changed only by the slow change of the eyes throughout time everlasting.'

Another Norfolk hotel guest was a man who lassoed lion and rhino with a 30 ft-long lariat to parade them through Nairobi. Yet another regular at the Norfolk — later it attracted such famous writers as Ernest Hemingway, Negley Farson, Baroness Karen Blixen who wrote that Kenya classic *Out of Africa*, Elspeth Huxley and Alan Moorehead — was an eccentric who hunted lion with a pack of hounds whom he urged on with cries of 'Tally-ho' and blasts on a silver horn.

Around this period, the young Winston Churchill visited Kenya in his capacity as Britain's Under-Secretary of State for the Colonies. He donned a dark blue safari suit and sun-helmet to ride the railway from Mombasa to

Nairobi through 'the biggest natural zoological gardens in the world'.

During the sixteen-hour journey, he sat on a park bench mounted over the cow (elephant?) catcher of the locomotive and took pot-shots with a sporting rifle at the Cape buffalo, lion and gazelles scattered over the savannah around him. He wrote later that the railway was 'an iron fact, grinding along through the jungle and the plain, waking with its whistles the silence of the Nyanza and startling the tribes out of their primordial nakedness'.

Nairobi railway station was then but a wooden platform with a corrugated iron roof and a kitchen clock suspended from the doorway. The clock was of little account as the trains were invariably late.

When the Great War broke out between England and Germany in August, 1914, the majority of Kenya's British settlers left their farmlands to volunteer for military service.

They went off to fight in a long and arduous East African campaign against the forces of General Paul von Lettow-Vorbeck, a brilliant and chivalrous German commander who constantly outwitted the Allies with his guerrilla tactics.

The Kenyan volunteer units were as bizarre as their men, 'Monica's Own' and 'Bowker's Horse' being but two of them. The gallants of the latter regiment were ignominiously defeated, far from a battlefield, when the Germans stole their mounts!

Two years after the 1918 armistice, the British Government declared Kenya a colony — but subsequently rejected the whites' demands for 'informal self-government' and declared 'the interests of the African natives must be paramount'.

The settlers smiled wryly, and went on building their own world. Their agricultural development of the colony continued doggedly between the two world wars despite diseases fatal to man or beast such as malaria, rinderpest, sleeping sickness and foot-and-mouth. The farmers also battled against crop pests, locusts, creeping thorn-brush, rampaging wild animals, seasons of drought when water was more precious than gold, and a long list of other menaces.

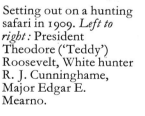

Setting out on a hunting safari in 1909. *Left to right:* President Theodore ('Teddy') Roosevelt, White hunter R. J. Cunninghame, Major Edgar E. Mearno.

Some small, secondary industries were established around Nairobi and Mombasa. 'We grafted a growing modern civilization on to untutored Africans who have since become leaders in politics, business, the arts and the professions', claims one of the 'old hands' from England.

It was during the long lull in international conflict that African political consciousness began to grow — while the country, with its glorious scenery, temperate climate, lack of servant problems and many opportunities for an easy life, attracted a host of high-born philanderers and was dubbed 'a place in the sun for shady people'. And when the Second World War broke out in September 1939, Kenya's blue-blood 'Happy Valley' set, far from the perils of total war, ran wild, brazenly violating the sexual mores of the time.

Men more patriotic or less fortunate signed up to fight the Italians in next-door Ethiopia.

With the end of the war in 1945, the agitation by soil-hungry tribespeople in Kenya for *uhuru* (freedom) was heightened by the return from abroad to their ethnic reserves of African ex-servicemen who had tasted democracy and seen wider horizons. Now the bleak prospect before them was unemployment in a country where there was a grave shortage of subsistence land and prices for food, clothing and other essentials were rocketing.

A middle-aged Jomo Kenyatta, who had spent the war years in embattled Britain as a socialist lecturer, agricultural labourer and an extra in African jungle films, returned to his native Kenya in 1946 to co-ordinate and lead a movement pledged to overthrow colonial rule.

Kenyatta, who as a boy had herded cattle and goats in rural Ichaweri, was a spell-binder as an orator. He would delight his listeners at public meetings with snide remarks in Swahili or Kikuyu directed against the white masters, or would indicate with a clockwise twirl of his ivory-handled fly-whisk that he meant the exact opposite of what he was saying.

While the white-dominated farming economy of the country was booming, the Africans, principally Kenyatta's Kikuyu who were the biggest and most influential tribe, had reached a state of revolt. Incensed by continued white appropriation of agricultural land while their demands were, by and large, ignored, the Africans were by now convinced they could only obtain *uhuru* through force.

The Mau Mau rebellion broke out early in 1952, shortly after Elizabeth II had become Queen of England overnight in Kenya when her father, King George VI, died as she was watching elephants and other wild game from a platform set high in the branches of a tree in the Aberdare forest.

The British declared a 'state of emergency' on war lines in October 1952. Kenyatta and other black leaders were imprisoned and he was later 'rusticated' under armed guard in harsh semi-desert country.

Fighters in a rag-tag Mau Mau army attacked both black Kenyans suspected of disloyalty to their cause and some whites. Bestial oathing ceremonies were forced on kidnapped victims.

Thousands on either side were to die in ghastly circumstances before the rebellion was put down and Kenyatta freed. The official death-count was 13,000 black Kenyans, mostly Kikuyu, and 32 Europeans. The Mau Mau lost 11,503 men and women, and a total of 80,000 dissidents were confined to British concentration camps during the Emergency.

After nearly a decade of bloodshed and terror, the British conceded that independence for the indigenous peoples of Kenya's 225,000 square miles of territory was inevitable.

The late Jomo Kenyatta

At a midnight ceremony in Nairobi on 12th December 1963, the Union Jack was hauled down in the glare of a searchlight amid thunderous cheers.

'I snatched you out of the lion's belly,' Kenyatta told an exulting crowd of Africans a year later when he became the first president of a Kenya republic.

Taking account of the Africans' hunger for education, he introduced an inspired system whereby the people built their own schools and the government provided the equipment and the teachers.

He kept British advisers and technicians in his administration until they wanted to return home or could be replaced by Africans. His government bought out land in the former 'White Highlands' to hand over to black peasant farmers.

Although a white missionary had once accused his father of being a witchdoctor, he urged foreign churchmen of all denominations – and expatriate businessmen – to stay on in independent Kenya.

Over the years of freedom, Mzee (Grand Old Man) Kenyatta boldly met the challenges of black Africa's four main problems – poverty, ignorance, disease and unemployment.

He turned his back on divisive racialism, corrosive bitterness and narrow tribalism.

His creed was: 'It is the future that is living and the past that is dead.'

He borrowed from the black crewmen who hauled on the ropes of river-ferry rafts the rallying call of *Harambee* – 'Let's all pull together'.

When he died in his sleep in Mombasa in August 1978, the octogenarian 'Father of Kenya' had made his green and pleasant land a model of multiracial peace and progress in an otherwise turbulent Africa. His name and influence live on.

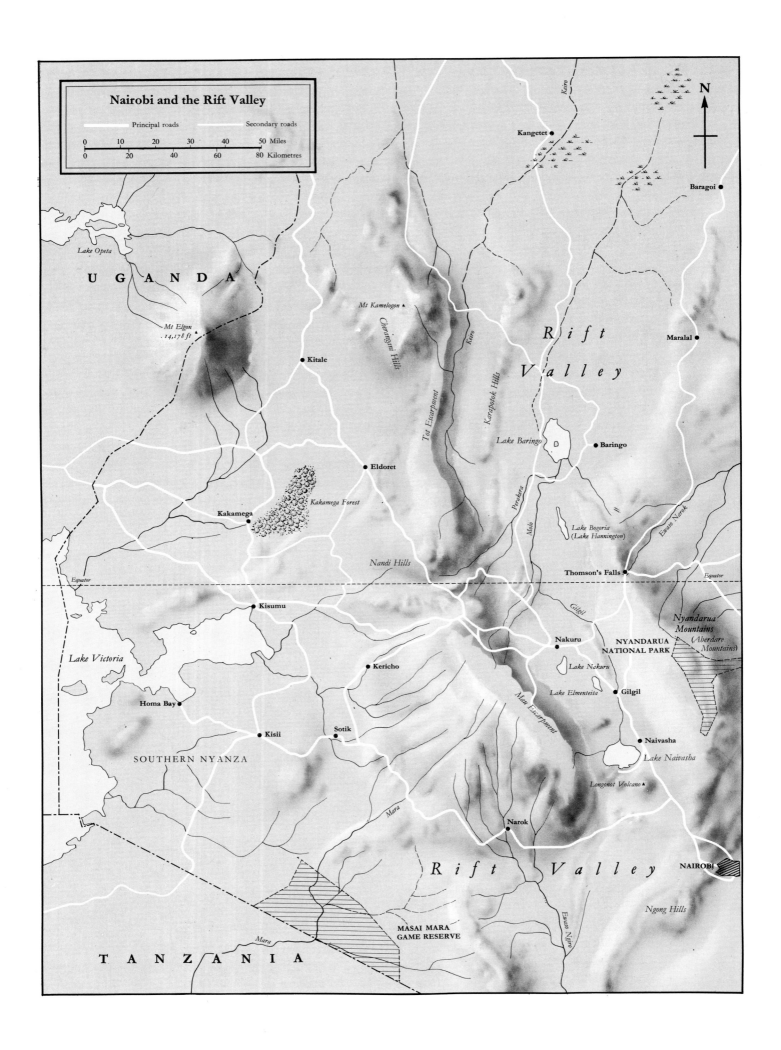

Nairobi and the Rift Valley

Principal roads   Secondary roads

0	10	20	30	40	50	Miles
0	20	40	60	80		Kilometres

N

UGANDA

Lake Opeta

*Mt Elgon
· 14,178 ft* ▲

Kitale

Cherangani Hills

Mt Kamelogon ▲

Kangetet ●

Baragoi ●

Tot Escarpment

R i f t

V a l l e y

Maralal ●

Kerio

Kerio

Karapokok Hills

Lake Baringo

Baringo ●

Eldoret ●

Kakamega Forest

Kakamega ●

Perakra

Molo

*Lake Bogoria
(Lake Hannington)*

Ewaso Narok

Nandi Hills

Thomson's Falls ●

Equator

Equator

Kisumu ●

Gilgil

*Nyandarua
Mountains
(Aberdare
Mountains)*

Nakuru ●

**NYANDARUA
NATIONAL PARK**

Lake Victoria

Kericho ●

Lake Nakuru

Lake Elmenteita

Gilgil ●

Homa Bay ●

Mau Escarpment

Naivasha ●

Kisii ●

Sotik ●

Lake Naivasha

SOUTHERN NYANZA

Longonot Volcano ▲

Mara

Narok ●

R i f t   V a l l e y

NAIROBI

Ewaso Ngiro

Ngong Hills

Mara

**MASAI MARA
GAME RESERVE**

T A N Z A N I A

2

The Rift Valley and the Lakes

Proclaimed a city by King George VI in 1950, Nairobi is today black Africa's leading business centre, the main springboard to the country's gamelands, and the conservation capital of the world.

From that handful of white trail-blazers three-quarters of a century ago, the mixed race population of Nairobi — Africans, Asians and Europeans — has grown to 850,000.

The city's avenues and parks, lined with flowering trees, shrubs and tropical blooms, are a kaleidoscope of colour and beauty. Characterised by architecture of striking grace and modernistic range, Nairobi has become the hub of black Africa and headquarters of the United Nations Environment Programme (UNEP) which has set itself the monumental task of saving the earth from the ravages of man.

Her sunny streets are thronged with tourists from America and Europe who wear neatly-pressed safari suits of blue or khaki and sport bush-hats with (plastic) 'leopard-skin' bands. Black hustlers press on them 'elephant hair' bracelets guaranteed to protect the wearer from a charging rogue elephant. Again, the 'magic' bracelet is merely plastic and will only save its owner from plastic elephants.

Bearded Sikhs in turbans mingle with black-haired Asian girls in flowing, rainbow-hued saris in the 'City of Flowers'.

Grinning Samburu warriors with flame-coloured togas flung over their shoulders point their spears at a painting of a roaring lion in the window of a city art gallery as Western-suited African and Japanese businessmen stroll by, statutory well-worn briefcases under their arms.

Arab dhow sailors up from Mombasa flirt with ebony-skinned Kenyan girls wearing their gaily-patterned dresses and high-heeled shoes.

British airline stewardesses haggle with the pavement sellers of convoluted carvings of wood and vegetable ivory.

The Kenyan capital, where for the greater part of every year it is comfortably warm by day and the nights are refreshingly cool, is dominated by East Africa's tallest building — the circular, 440 ft. high Kenyatta Conference Centre that cost £4 million and has 28 storeys. Looking something like a giant hair-curler under a sunshade, the KCC is the conference venue of global organisations such as the International Monetary Fund, the World Council of Churches, and UNCTAD. Thousands of delegates can be seated in the vast plenary session hall with its olive-wood panels, soft lighting and flags of all nations.

The top floor of the Conference Centre slowly revolves at night, giving an aerial view of the silvered cupolas of the city's mosques, the imposing, white-walled university, the amber-glowing Hilton hotel (another skyscraper), the red-bricked Anglican cathedral, the casino on Las Vegas lines on Ainsworth Hill, the cinemas, theatres, night clubs, restaurants to suit all tastes and pockets, and the candlelit Thorn Tree pavement café, that well-known Pan-African meeting place in the heart of Nairobi.

The Thorn Tree is set on one of the capital's most fashionable main streets, named after independence by Kenyatta's government in memory of Kimathi, a Mau Mau leader who was captured and hanged by the British in 1955.

The original thorn tree at the site — there is now another that forms a green canopy over the patrons — was used as notice board by white hunters who pinned messages for their friends and clients on its greenish-yellow trunk.

Today the lower section of the tree is surrounded by a four-sided wooden board on which hitchhikers and passing romantics leave such appeals as 'Lift wanted to Cairo', and 'See you at Petley's Inn, Lamu, next Thursday.' Diners and drinkers at the Thorn Tree, which is part of the well-known New Stanley Hotel, range from film stars to hippies, safari guides to novelists in search of local colour, from tourists and tycoons to weirdly-garbed medicine men and former white hunters made idle by a government ban on the sport shooting of game animals. It is said, with some justification, that if you sit long enough at the Thorn Tree you are bound to meet an old friend from somewhere around the globe.

Although thorn trees (acacias) are also called fever trees on account of the diseases contracted by people camping under them in the early days — they often grew near lakes and swamps, the breeding grounds of mosquitoes — it is highly unlikely the visitor will contract malaria while drinking a 'Tusker' beer at the Thorn Tree.

Not far away 'Entry With Shoes Strictly Prohibited' declares a sign over the door of the Sunni sect's mosque — three cupolas and two minarets — in the centre of a cosmopolitan city that also boasts a 'Royal Scottish Country Dance Society' and has regular race meetings with barefoot black jockeys, bearded Asian bookmakers, blanketed punters, and owners with red carnations in their buttonholes leaning on shooting sticks.

Near the mosque, packed with Moslems on a Friday, is Kenya's National Theatre where both Africans and Europeans stage productions. While the latter might present *My Fair Lady* or *Guys and Dolls* in a neat little theatre whose foyer has a stone from the house where Shakespeare was born, the African plays feature grotesquely-masked figures from folklore tales or heroes of the Mau Mau Rebellion.

The National Theatre is overlooked by the National Museum that is of special interest even for visitors who normally steer clear of such institutions. It is closely associated with the Leakey family of palaeontologists whose work, as a related group, to solve the riddles of man's origins is unrivalled.

While the museum's exhibits vary from relics of prehistoric man to half ostrich-egg-shells used to cover the navals of circumcised single women when they are dancing, a stout-walled vault deep in its pastoral grounds houses a half-skull — brain cover, eye sockets and upper jaw — that is unique on earth and beyond price.

The skull has the mundane tag of '1470', merely a number in the museum's catalogue, but its discoverer, Richard Leakey, the young director of

Kenya's National Museums, believes it is the skull of a 'handy man' (or woman) known as *Homo habilis* who lived in northern Kenya around two million years ago. His find caused a sensation in the scientific world.

Only a cast of '1470' – which was put together painstakingly from about 300 pieces of fossilised bone unearthed by Leakey in 1972 – is on view to the public in the museum itself.

In the Nairobi Snake Park opposite the museum, notices are as effectively ghoulish as the residents – cobras, pythons and puff-adders – and fascinating in their menacing fashion. A warning over one snake-pit reads: 'Trespassers Will Be Poisoned'. Visitors to a section containing crocodiles 12 to 15 ft. long are told that anyone throwing litter into the water will be required to retrieve it!

A huge elephant with long, sweeping tusks confronts people leaving the Snake Park, a taxidermist's reconstruction in artificial skin and false ivory of 'Ahmed', monarch of the forests of Marsabit, who died peacefully after being protected for many years from poachers and hunters under a special decree issued by President Kenyatta. King-sized Ahmed was regarded as the world's most magnificent elephant.

There are no elephants in Nairobi National Park, but most other East African wild animals can be seen there at one time or another. It is just five miles from the city centre.

In 1900, Lord Delamere was the first person to suggest the creation of wildlife reserves in Kenya, and there are now more than thirty of them. But 46 years passed before his proposal was acted upon as a result of a 13-year campaign, interrupted by the Second World War, on the part of a would-be white hunter who turned conservationist before picking up a rifle: courtly Mervyn Cowie.

On Christmas Eve 1946, Nairobi National Park, the first of its kind in Kenya, was gazetted, and Cowie was appointed director.

Three sides of the 44 square mile sanctuary are fenced, but the southern end is left open in order to allow the animals free access to and from extensive adjacent areas, like the Athi Plain, that form natural game reservoirs. Another free-ranging area for the animals is provided by the grey, knuckle-shaped Ngong Hills that overlook Nairobi. There is a Maasai legend that the lion, the rhino and the other big beasts turned down an appeal to rid the people of a murderous ogre. But the ants got together and suffocated the sleeping giant in earth, leaving only the knuckles of one hand bare. Another of the many legends woven around the Ngong Hills is that they are the earth God flicked from his fingers at the end of Creation.

Isak Dinesen, the pen-name of Karen Blixen after whom a wealthy Nairobi suburb is named, wrote that the rocky Ngong area, rich in game, 'had not its like in all the world'. Her big game hunter lover, who was killed in a plane crash, is buried in the hills that overlooked the writer's coffee farm.

During a two-hour drive in the Nairobi Game Park (with the screen of an open-air cinema and beyond that the shimmering outline of Nairobi itself as dropcloths), visitors may see a wide variety of wild animals in their natural state – lion, leopard, rhino, cheetah, hippo, Cape buffalo, giraffe, zebra, wildebeest and large herds of other plains game.

A baboon squats on top of a wooden signpost that reads 'Beware of the Crocodiles', and a female cheetah and her three cubs gnaw with bloodied muzzles on the foreleg of a gazelle she had run down and killed an hour before as a blood-red sun rose over Nairobi's crenellated skyline.

Ringed by cars and Land-Rovers, a pride of lion lies sprawled under an 'umbrella tree', blinking lazily in the filtered sunlight. They are majestically indifferent to the cameras clicking and whirring round them.

Lions are among the greatest attractions of the park and the regular question asked at its gate is 'Wapi simba?' — 'Where are the lions?'. These are generally pin-pointed for new arrivals, seeking souvenir shots of gambolling cubs, by clusters of cars in some part of the park.

In such a near-urban setting, it is hard for one to believe that these and other big game are savage wild animals — the inevitable dear old lady will want to clamber out of the zebra-striped minibus to pick up and fondle an ostrich chick. So the park's rules are strictly enforced by touring wardens and game scouts. Roof-hatches of safari vehicles must remain closed, cars must not leave the tracks, and bitumenised humps enforce a 20 m.p.h. speed limit. Entry to the park later than an hour before dark is forbidden.

The best times to view the animals are soon after sunrise as they return to the bush from hunting or foraging expeditions, or late afternoon when they emerge after the heat of the day to drink at the park's waterholes.

There is a small forest area in the northern part of the park, but the greater portion consists of open grassy plains transected by water-courses and wooded ravines.

The park protects some eighty species, and has a bird population bigger than Britain's.

Next to the main gate is the Animal Orphanage, founded at the time of independence to tend and rehabilitate wildlife waifs who lose their parents through poachers, predators, accident or disease. Although young or sick animals have to be kept in cages until they can fend for themselves and are set free, a sign at the entrance to the 25-acre orphanage states: 'This Is Not a Zoo'.

Its transient intakes might include a young leopard found in a steelwire snare, or cheetah cubs abandoned in the wild.

A toothless circus lion was a permanent resident of the novel orphanage until he died peacefully of old age within hearing of the deep-throated roars of his relatives who were born free. Other residents are a couple of rare pygmy hippos, a gift from the West African state of Liberia.

First on the itinerary of most tourists after Nairobi National Park is a drive along the spectacular road clinging to the side of the Rift Valley. From the top of the escarpment one has a superb panoramic view of part of the 4,000-mile long Rift that formed East Africa's inverted backbone some thirty million years ago.

Past the extinct volcano of Longonot is Lake Naivasha, fed by springs deep in the earth. It is the weekend playground for Nairobi people who sail dinghies on its temperamental waters, fish for the tenacious black bass, join bird-watching expeditions to see pelicans and Goliath herons among the reeds, papyrus and waterlilies, or just laze in the tropical sun on its shores. Schools of hippos, nearly four times the size of their pygmy cousins in the Nairobi Orphanage, also attract international travellers as well as local picnic parties to Lake Naivasha.

The lake, which was discovered by a German naturalist in 1883, rises and falls, shrinks or expands, according to the rainfall. Its original outlet was probably the appropriately named 'Hell's Gate', a rocky gorge with impressive cliffs which afford nesting places to lammergeyers (bearded vultures).

Lake Naivasha is a home of a variety of birds including the handsome fish-eagle with its shrill, haunting cry, black wings, tan-coloured frontage and imperious white head. The lake also supplies crayfish — small lobster-like fresh-water crustaceans — to Nairobi's luxury hotels and restaurants.

Several well-known Kenya residents have attractive homes among the thorn trees that ring Lake Naivasha. Among them was the late Joy Adamson. The American television version of her *Born Free* story of Elsa the lioness was filmed there.

Forty miles on from Naivasha, through Gilgil that was once the centre of Kenya's 'Happy Valley' crowd, lies Nakuru, centre of some of the country's richest farmland.

The African version of a sleepy market town, it is regarded as the farming capital of Kenya, but its alkaline Rift Valley lake is the setting for what has been described by experts as 'the greatest ornithological spectacle on earth'.

The lake's microscopic plants or algae attract multitudes of flamingoes — up to a million at a time — and turn its shoreline into a huge, dazzling 'rose garden'.

Apart from the world's greatest population of these graceful and attractive birds, there are more than four hundred other species — cormorants perched on dead trees like etchings, hovering sunbirds sipping nectar, and pelicans floating in line ahead, dipping their pouches deep to scoop up fingerlings of bream — that led Britain's Sir Peter Scott to declare: 'Nakuru is the finest bird lake I have ever seen.'

Some sixty miles beyond Nakuru, high above the floor of the Rift, are great, green tea plantations dotted with black men and women pickers in their waterproof jackets of bright yellow (for here it rains, sometime, every day) carrying wicker baskets on their backs.

Kericho, pronounced 'ke-reech-o', has been the centre of Kenya's tea estates that serve both foreign and local markets since the first bush was planted in 1906.

In mountain streams around the town, there is excellent trout-fishing with wet or dry flies that have been made by teams of handicapped Africans.

It is the country of the long-legged Kipsigis, a once-pastoral tribe that, alongside the Kalenjin group has produced many of Kenya's top-class athletes.

According to Kipsigi legend, the Nandi Hills, another tea-growing district, are the abode of an African 'yeti' they call the 'Nandi Bear'. A soft-footed monster disguised as an hyena, the Nandi Bear is believed to live in a house deep in a forest, stalking his victims at night and tearing off their heads after beating them to death with a cudgel. Another version is that the bear speaks local tongues and, having turned itself into a Kipsigi, joins a party of tribespeople to select some unfortunate, luring him or her away before making his deadly attack. A clay cookpot carried on the head at night is believed to be strong *ju ju* against the Nandi Bear.

In the hills live the proud Nandi people who were fierce opponents of British rule.

The Dorobo of this part of Kenya, who still carry bows and arrows, are survivors of the aboriginal inhabitants of the country and are believed by the Nandi to have been the original people on earth.

Renowned hunters and trackers, they are particularly fond of wild honey and have established a remarkable relationship with the honey-bird that guides them to swarms of wild bees in the trees. Having smoked out the bees, the

sweet-toothed Dorobo break open the combs and remove most of the honey —
always leaving, however, a generous portion for the small birds that led them
to the prize.

One of the most splendid spectacles in western Kenya is the regular 'regatta'
out of Kisumu by the Nilotic Luo bream-fishermen of Lake Victoria. The
triangular sails of their canoes fill with wind as they paddle furiously. The
competitors shoot across the grey-green surface of the world's second largest
freshwater lake to be cheered home — the winner gets a goat for his prize — by a
boisterous and ululating throng on the reedy banks.

Sweltering Kisumu, the third largest town in Kenya, was Port Florence
when the railroad from Mombasa reached it in December 1901. It is the
headquarters of the Luo, the country's second largest tribe, to whom the town's
name means 'Where one goes to get one's needs'.

The Luo, who wear a ceremonial dress of black-and-white Colobus monkey
skins, python bones and hippo teeth, exploit the fish resources of an island sea
250 miles long and 200 miles wide, but the tribe has also provided many of
Kenya's best scientists, politicians and doctors.

The Kisii tribespeople who live in southern Nyanza, the old name for lake,
are settled agriculturalists whose medicine men still practise a primitive form
of trepanning for headache and madness, exposing the skull and removing a
circular section of bone to allow an evil spirit to escape from the brain.

Kakamega forest, 30 miles from Kisumu, is botanically West African and
chiefly notable for its large snake and bird populations together with gigantic
horned beetles, exotic butterflies and the black and white casqued hornbill.

Kakamega town, focal point of one of Kenya's most densely populated
areas, was the scene some fifty years ago of a short-lived gold rush. Despite the
Klondike fever, only small quantities of gold were panned, and today most
signs of mining operations there have disappeared.

Elephant, buffalo, rhino and Colobus monkeys inhabit the thick bamboo
forests above the 8,000 ft. contour of austere Mount Elgon in north-west
Kenya on the edge of the country's lush farming areas.

Mount Elgon's volcanic crater, four miles across, is one of the largest of its
kind in Africa. Among Mount Elgon's foothills are caves of cathedral proportions containing thousands of bats that form a dark cloud against the dying sun
as they emerge each evening.

Between Mount Elgon and Lake Baringo are the Cherangani Hills, a major
mountain range, crystalline not volcanic, that forms part of the Great Rift
Valley's western wall.

Kamelogon (11,540 ft.) is the highest peak of the Cheranganis that, like
Mount Kenya, have moorlands of giant heath (*Erica arborea*).

From the Tot escarpment there are breathtaking vistas all around, over the
brooding sweep of the Rift Valley, Kenya's main geological feature, and across
to the Karapokot Hills. But the landscape is veiled in ash-blue smoke,
testifying as elsewhere in Kenya to the ravaging of indigenous forests for wood
to be burned into charcoal used by the tribespeople for cooking. There is not a
single lump of coal to be found in the country, and so the disastrous plunder of
the woodlands goes on.

Richard Leakey's elder brother, Jonathan, has 1,500 snakes of nine species
on his serum farm at Lake Baringo, north of Nakuru. Jonathan captures and
milks the deadly snakes for their venom used in snakebite serum.

Kenya's president, Daniel arap Moi, who succeeded Kenyatta, is a member of the small Tugen tribe that uses frail reed boats for fishing among the hippo and crocodiles of Lake Baringo.

Baringo's sister-lake, Hannington (now re-named Bogoria) was named after Bishop James Hannington of England's Church Missionary Society who was murdered on the orders of the Kabaka of Buganda at a Nile crossing in 1885. Lake Bogoria, covering only 13 square miles, has a small flamingo population, but it is known chiefly for its hot sulphur springs, steam jets and thermal geysers from which boiling water erupts; all part of a harsh moon-scape.

On the other hand Thomson's Falls (now known as Nyahuru) consist of broad, icy ribbons of 200,000 gallons of river-water plunging 237 ft. into a gorge that is flanked by a tangled tropical forest.

The Falls were named after his father by the Scottish explorer, Joseph Thomson from Dumfries, who came upon them in his travels in 1883. Thomson also gives his name to one of Kenya's best-known and attractive wild creatures, the Thomson's gazelle with its satiny rufous-brown coat and a blackish-brown lateral strip dividing the upper flank from the white belly. The Africans call it *swala tomi*. Roast or marinated haunches of 'Tommy' are a feature of some Kenya hotels.

In the vicinity of the Falls, at 9,000 ft., there is a high-altitude training camp for Kenya's black athletes. For many of these, the remote waterfall has been the starting point for a triumphal career at the Olympic Games.

Parliament buildings and Kenyatta Conference Centre

Jacaranda trees, Jeevanjee Gardens

Kenyatta Avenue

NAIROBI NATIONAL PARK   Young cheetah

Opposite: Baboons drinking, spotted hyena and wildebeest

Above: Flamingo at Lake Nakuru – Africa's finest bird lake
Left: Dusk at Lake Naivasha, pelicans roosting on a tree
Below: Sail boat on Lake Victoria

Crested Cranes in flight

View over the Rift Valley from near Kaptegat

Tea pickers in the Kericho district

Tea estate at Subukia

Sifting coffee beans at a coffee co-operative near Kiambu

An old Dorobo on the Mau escarpment

Nandi boy in circumcision paint

Landscape in the Nandi Hills

A Nandi elder

Oxen ploughing team in the Nandi Hills

Sisal growing near Homa Bay

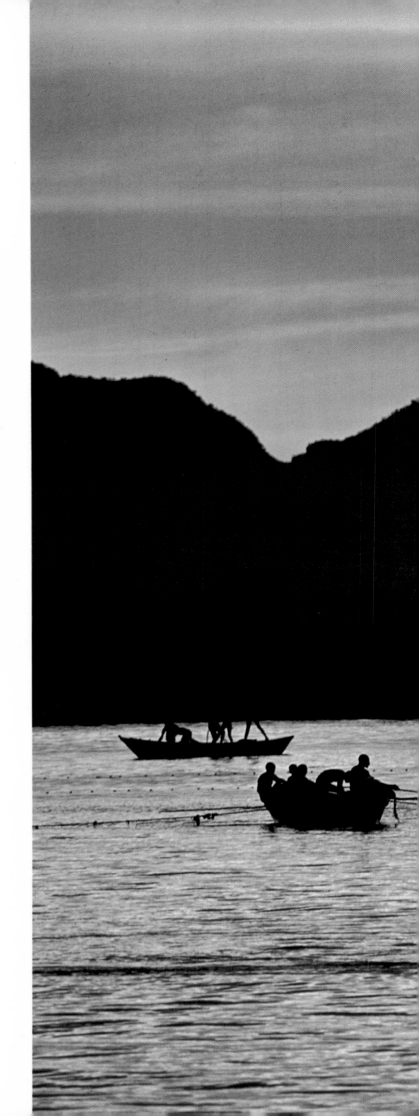

Dusk at Lake Victoria – Luo fishermen in Kendu Bay

Luo fishing boats
returning to
Dunga village,
Lake Victoria

Market at Magunga, South Nyanza

Luo village near Chemelil, Nyanza

Luo woman making clay pots

Luo clay pots at Kisumu market

Left: Clerodendrum myricoides
Below left: Amplexi caulis
Below: Momordica foetida, fruit

Right: Verreaux's Eagle owl in a fever tree
Far right: Malachite sunbird
Below right: Superb starling
Below far right: Taveta Golden weaver

Grey heron – just caught a frog!

Njemp girl carrying reeds, Lake Baringo

Old woman on a dusty road, Elgeyo escarpment

Young crocodiles

Monitor lizard eating fish

Flamingo on Lake Bogoria – hot springs in foreground

Hot springs at Lake Bogoria

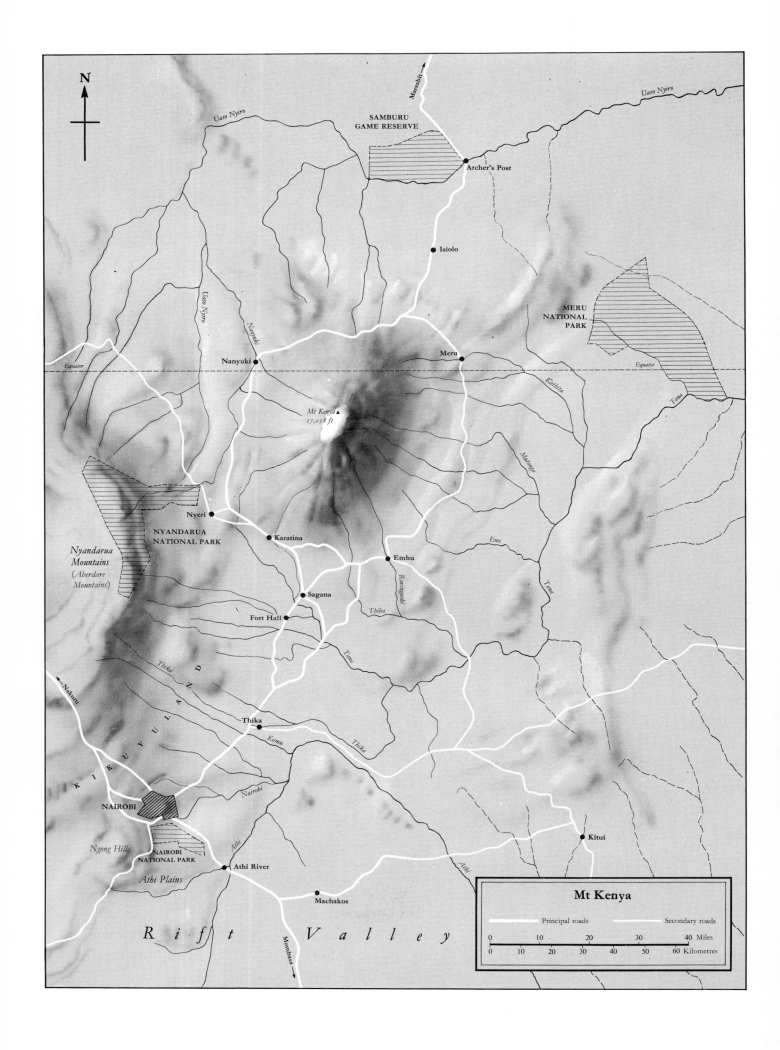

N

SAMBURU
GAME RESERVE

Uaso Nyiro

Marsabit

Archer's Post

Uaso Nyiro

Isiolo

MERU
NATIONAL
PARK

Nanyuki

Equator

Meru

Equator

Kathita

Tana

Mt Kenya ▲
17,058 ft

Matongi

Nyeri

NYANDARUA
NATIONAL PARK

Karatina

Ena

Nyandarua
Mountains
(Aberdare
Mountains)

Embu

Sagana

Ramingatbi

Tana

Thiba

Fort Hall

Tana

K I K U Y U L A N D

Thika

Thika

Nakuru

Thika

Komu

Thika

Nairobi

NAIROBI

Ngong Hills

NAIROBI
NATIONAL PARK

Athi

Kitui

Athi River

Athi Plains

Athi

Machakos

R   i   f   t   V   a   l   l   e   y

Mombasa

Mt Kenya

Principal roads   Secondary roads

0		10		20		30		40 Miles
0	10	20	30	40	50	60 Kilometres		

3

Around the Mountain

Lying in a tranquil, verdant valley between two mountain ranges, little Nyeri, a hundred miles from Nairobi, is the heart and soul of Kikuyuland and as such the farmlands and forests around it were the principal strongholds of the Mau Mau rebels of the fifties.

Kikuyu folklore has it that the nine daughters of a couple named Gikuyu and Mumbi were the founders of the nine-clan tribe that spread out along the ridges and valleys of the Aberdare Mountains (now called Nyandarua) to become Kenya's dominant African people – administrators, traders, farmers and teachers, scattered all over the country with Mount Kenya as their spiritual shrine.

For all that, the majority of Kikuyu women, daughters of *the* daughters, still await emancipation. Although proud of their heavy loads, they present a sad and harrowing sight for female liberationists as they stagger along country roads with up to 200 lbs. of firewood, supported by a head-thong, on their bent backs.

A little more than fifty years ago, Nyeri had a population of nine wheat farmers and coffee planters from Britain. One of the first things they did, of course, was to lay out an 18-hole golf course, and one of their number built a four-bedroom hotel with the latest modern convenience – a water closet. Yet another pioneer brought in brown trout of the Loch Levan variety and stocked the sparkling streams of the Nyandaruas. Trout fishing there and elsewhere in Kenya is still one of the best bargains one can buy – 30p or five Kenyan shillings for a 48-hour permit.

The tiny Nyeri hostelry grew into a rambling country mansion surrounded by towering eucalyptus trees and port-wine coloured bougainvillaea bushes. It is now the Outspan Hotel.

Lord Robert Baden-Powell, Chief Scout of the world, spent his last days in a steep-roofed cottage named 'Paxtu' attached to the hotel. The 'Hero of Mafeking' in the Anglo-Boer War believed 'the nearer to Nyeri, the nearer to bliss'.

Baden-Powell died at eighty-three in January 1941 and was buried in the town cemetery near the grave of the 'Boy's Own Paper' big-game hunter, Jim Corbett. The founder of the Scout movement's headstone bears the 'Gone home' trail sign of a circle with a dot in the middle, and 'Paxtu' is visited in pilgrimage every year by hundreds of Scouts and Guides of all colours.

Above the mantelpiece of 'Paxtu', preserved as a Scouting memorial to B.P., is a framed copy of his last Christmas card that he designed himself and sent out to thousands of friends in the darkest days of the Second World War. 'Have courage in the face of war, and fight on for better days of peace', he wrote.

The Outspan is the starting point for an overnight visit to Treetops Lodge that has become synonymous with Africa around the world.

Treetops was first mooted in the early thirties by Lady Bettie Fielding, with memories of Peter Pan and a treehouse built back in England by her brothers and sisters. She and her husband decided to build the 'Wendy House' because they felt it would encourage people to shoot animals with cameras, not guns. Big game hunting by kings and wealthy captains of industry was then at its height in East Africa.

Treetops began humbly as a two-room log cabin in a wild fig tree, sacred to the Kikuyu, in the Aberdare forest. The first two guests, who climbed a long ladder to reach their game-viewing perch, came in November 1932. The tree was ringed with barbed wire to keep off leopards and lions.

One of the early occupants of the original timber Treetops, the author R. O. Pearse, wrote dramatically of his first night there: 'It was bitterly cold. Then the fun started. First the forest began to rustle all around us, and then came the trampling of heavy beasts. Every now and then came the scream of an elephant, cutting the darkness like a whiplash; strange grunts and snortings. And then the whole orchestra started in full blast. The row was indescribable — every form of unearthly yell, screech, snort, howl, cry you can imagine. Some were like a long-drawn sob, others like the moan of a soul in torment; then there would come a savage snarl, or terrified shriek, and then silence, broken by heavy snortings, and deep breathing immediately below us. Safe as we were, we didn't feel too happy. It was the most eerie of all our experiences.'

The next day he took up his story again: 'As dawn broke, silence fell, and when we got up, nothing but heaps of dung and trampled grass and broken branches of trees remained to tell of the midnight orgies of the denizens of the forest.'

Back at the Outspan, the author recalled: 'The hotel proprietor told us a graphic story of how the place was built. Every day the rhinos would come out and charge the builder, and every time they charged, the builder put up his price!'

Guests at Treetops in its early years included Tsar Ferdinand of Bulgaria; the Duke and Duchess of Gloucester; Earl Mountbatten; Queen Elizabeth, the Queen Mother; and Mr and Mrs Neville Chamberlain.

On the evening in February 1952, when Princess Elizabeth and her husband, Prince Philip, arrived to spend a night there, the royal couple were menaced by a restless cow elephant guarding her young. She blocked the way to the lodge ladder, and flapped her ears irritably as if preparing to charge.

'I had sometimes taken people along the path to Treetops when elephants were about, but never at such close quarters as this', said the armed guide later. 'The princess did not falter. She walked straight towards the elephant, and smiled a greeting to my wife who was waiting halfway down the ladder. Then unhurriedly she handed my wife her handbag and camera and climbed the steep ladder.'

The next morning, when the English girl had left and become Queen of England on the death of her father, the guide paced out the distance between the foot of the ladder and the imprint of the nearest elephant's forefeet. It came to just under eight steps.

Treetops was burned down by the Mau Mau two years after the royal visit, and later a much larger, three-storey version was built close by, overlooking a large clearance in the middle of which is a waterhole 'baited' with blocks of salt and floodlit at night by an 'artificial moon'. Elephant could be seen taking mudslides into the water on their great behinds— and obviously enjoying every moment of the new sport. Treetops can now sleep nearly a hundred visitors, and has two VIP suites.

Another equally novel but more modern game lodge in the Nyandaruas is The Ark, designed from local wood in the style of Noah's original but containing comforts and amenities unheard of in the old man's day.

The Space Age ark has an arching prow, a stout-panelled roof of which Noah would have been proud, and a drawbridge that is raised at night for the animals come to its illuminated waterhole in numbers that would have sent him into a tizzy of accounting. There are rhino, elephant, buffalo, the giant forest hog, waterbuck, the rare and lovely bongo (a shy forest antelope with spiralled horns, chestnut in colour with vertical cream stripes on its glossy flanks), or perhaps a black leopard.

The nearby Aberdare Salient, where Prince Charles camped on his last visit to East Africa, contains the largest surviving black rhino population in Kenya.

The Ark is surrounded by a sea of thick montane forest, but it is possible to stand there eyeball-to-eyeball with a patriarch elephant in perfect safety. A feature of the lodge — built on stilts or 'floats' of timber from around Mount Kenya— is a 'dungeon' discreetly built into the lodge at ground level. Through embrasures in the walls, visitors can get memorable close-up pictures in which it looks as though the photographer is shooting from the middle of a herd of elephants.

A less dramatic but equally coveted photographic souvenir can be shot before entering Nanyuki, or 'Red Water', once an important agricultural and safari town, surrounded by wheat and cattle farms that are now returning from white to African ownership. Reaching the boundary of Nanyuki from The Ark, stand astride the Equator line indicated by a signboard and — click! — there's a snap with a foot in each hemisphere.

Situated near Nanyuki, and claimed to be at the geographical centre of Kenya, is the elegant Mount Kenya Safari Club, 'instant Africa' for guests who have stepped out of the pages of *Debrett's Peerage, Who's Who* and lists of Hollywood 'Oscar' prizewinners.

The Club, also open to non-members at stiff daily fees, was originally a coffee farm whose European owner lived in a large, white-walled house facing Mount Kenya. The farm was sold when the coffee crop failed, and became a country hotel called Mawingo, the Kikuyu word for 'In the clouds'.

Early in 1959, American film star, William Holden, a Texas oilman and a Swiss banker bought Mawingo and founded the Mount Kenya Safari Club. Appropriately enough it now looks like a millionaire's manor house, set among 100 green acres where peacocks and crested cranes strut among the rose gardens and across the well-manicured lawns.

The Mawingo duckling was transformed into a commercial swan.

Charter members of the Club, given mounted golden elephants as souvenirs, had among their number Sir Winston Churchill, President Jomo Kenyatta, Prince Bernhard of the Netherlands, US President Lyndon Johnson, the Duke of Manchester, Conrad N. Hilton, William Randolph Hearst Jr., Bing Crosby and Bob Hope. In the visitors' book are the names of Clark Gable,

John Wayne, Trevor Howard, Sidney Poitier, Michael Caine, and other past and present screen stars, alongside such royal signatures as that of Prince Bertil of Sweden.

Long-term or daily members can rent a roses-round-the-door cottage, with a black-tiled sunken bath, or a garden suite among the flowering trees with a private bar, cedar-log fire and a luxuriously furnished lounge.

Other club amenities include a heated outdoor swimming pool with underground viewing ports as part of a cocktail bar, tennis courts, a nine-hole golf course and a pavilion, an airstrip, bowling green and riding stables. Zebroids, crosses between horses and zebra, can be hired as pack-animals for expeditions up Mount Kenya.

Entertainment is provided at lunchtime by a troupe of lively Chuka dancers in feathered head-dresses and black-and-white monkey skins who writhe and prance to the beat of jungle drums on a lawn below the terrace where a cold buffet – 'A little more caviar, sir?' – is served by white-coated waiters.

In June, 1977, the Club's assets and name were acquired by a company of private investors from Britain, America, Europe and the Middle East. Eventually Adnan Khashoggi, the international entrepeneur from Saudi Arabia, became the principal owner, and oil-rich sheiks and their veiled women joined the Club's safari elite.

Through the big picture windows of the trophy-decorated lounge, Mount Kenya with its snowy pinnacles and forested slopes appears as if in glorious Technicolour on a Panavision cinema screen, etched against a dazzling blue sky.

At 17,058 ft. it is Africa's second highest mountain (after Kilimanjaro), but geologists believe that as an active volcano several million years ago it was 6,000 ft. taller. When the inner holocaust died down, the volcano went into a state of decay, eroded by an immense icecap that extended down to the present forest level and by the snow and hail of the Pleistocene Ice Age. This left only the lava 'plugs', or spires, of Batian, Nelion and Lenana (who, like Nelion, was a witchdoctor) of a crater-less mountain.

Two hundred and fifty miles in circumference, Mount Kenya, said to be 'the world's most perfect model of an equatorial mountain' that is comparable to Mont Blanc and other great peaks of the Alps, rises from farmlands and savannah to bamboo jungle and thick forest; through a zone of moors and valleys, and then by way of lakes, glaciers and tarns to the peaks that offer stunning views of much of Kenya.

Major river systems emanate from the summits, cutting deep gorges through the moorland and forest regions into the farming areas on the plains. Most of the rivers abound with trout, and several hatcheries supply five-star Nairobi restaurants.

The mountain above the 11,000 ft. level is a national park of 227 square miles, a natural sanctuary for such wild animals as rhino, elephant and other big game among trees festooned with long streamers of lichen or 'Old Man's Beard'. Cape buffalo have been encountered at 15,000 ft. and lions seen on the misty upper moorland that looks like the cover of a science fiction magazine. Tree hyraxes, rat-like 'rabbits,' scream from a brown-barked 'tree' of giant groundsel, Afro-alpine heather appears as though seen through a powerful telescope at close quarters, and lobelia 15 ft. high seem like huge green cigars dotted with purple flowers. At twilight one has the sense of being surrounded by an army of towering beings from another planet.

Plantation forests share the more accessible lower slopes of the mountain and provide timber for regional sawmills. Among the wild fig trees and podocarpus are the leopard orchid and other rare flora.

Wheat farms in the dry northern foothills help provide Kenya's bread; rice fields and banana plantations flourish on the humid eastern plains; cattle ranches to the west provide prime beef; and tea plantations form dark-green patchworks on the southern slopes.

Since the tribe was born centuries ago, the Kikuyu have regarded Mount Kenya as the earthly throne of their god, Ngai, and his acolytes, hideous dwarfs called Gumbi.

Few people know the mountain better than Phil Snyder, an expert mountaineer and bush pilot, who has been the warden of its national park area for some years and has led the rescue of hundreds of climbers from all over the world who have been trapped among its upper peaks or injured by charging wild beasts in the forests of cedar and eucalyptus.

Something of a mystic himself, Warden Snyder is as fascinated by the mountain as the millions of Kikuyu who continue to hold *Kere Nyaga* in superstitious awe.

'Mount Kenya is snow on the Equator', he says, 'and for thousands of years none but the very holy dared enter this sanctuary of Ngai, the God of Creation.

'Strange and wonderful punishments were inflicted by Ngai in his rage against insolent intruders into his domain. His fury would make the sky darken, the clouds gather and the heavens tremble as he threw down rocks of ice upon their heads. He would take away a man's breath and leave him drowning in emptiness. Quietly, in the night, he would cause the water in gourds to become as solid as a rock.

'Many Kikuyu legends contain unscientific but nevertheless accurate descriptions of high-altitude phenomena to support the view that the snowline was occasionally visited by tribal holy men in the past. Even today my mountain rangers come across some gentle local man, or woman, who on a call from Ngai has walked alone, but unharmed, up through the forest and into the snowstorms of Batian or Nelion.

'On your own up there, it's easy to imagine you hear Ngai whispering above the blizzard. But it was probably only the gale moaning in the ice caves, or among the towering dead stems of bamboo.'

Or was it?

North-east of Mount Kenya is Meru National Park, home of the lioness Elsa of *Born Free*. Apart from some emerald swamplands in which the elephant appear like black boulders, the 700 square mile region is hot and dry but well supplied by nine palm-fringed rivers. While Meru town still has a 'Pig and Whistle' inn, the park's modern lodge has been build like a — chintzy — African mud hut village.

An enterprising and conservation-minded African district council gazetted Meru as a game reserve in 1959 after George Adamson, a warden, and his wife, Joy, erstwhile 'foster-parents' of Elsa and others of the famous lion family, had paced out the boundaries. Meru was the first wildlife sanctuary in Kenya to be established and managed by a black rural body.

It was in Meru that Joy and George Adamson, who had been obliged to shoot the lioness's man-eating mother, had cared for Elsa as an orphan and returned her to the wild from their camp on the Ura River.

Meru is also the home of some of Africa's animal curiosities like the blue-legged Somali ostrich; the agile, long-necked gerenuk gazelle that feeds in upstretched wallaby-fashion off tall bushes; and the liver-red reticulated giraffe with its crazy-paving markings.

The National Park was one of the last refuges of the white rhino, which is anything but white but has a wide lower lip — *weit* in Afrikaans, giving rise to the 'white' misnomer. The largest living land mammal after the elephant, the white rhino is a remarkably placid creature in contrast to the irascible black rhino. Meru game scouts could sometimes be seen herding their huge charges like dogs being taken for a walk in a London park.

The white rhino of Meru were captured in South Africa by game wardens firing darts containing a tranquilliser drug and shipped up to this Kenyan park where it was hoped to establish a vital new breeding ground for a gravely endangered species. Sadly most of them were killed by poachers soon after arriving in Meru.

The rutted high road out of Meru town, headquarters of the small tribe of that name, is notorious as one of the most gruelling sections of the annual 3,000 mile Kenya Safari, one of the roughest, toughest motor rallies in the world.

Some fifty miles further north, still within sight of Mount Kenya, a British elephant hunter, Arthur Neumann from Bedfordshire, made his camp where Samburu Game Lodge now stands in the animal reserve of that name. Neumann, the friend of other Victorian heroes of the African bush like Frederick Courteney Selous, Millais and Rowland Ward, came to old Kenya after tiring of a variety of jobs down south as a gold miner, coffee and cotton planter, an interpreter for a Swazi king and a magistrate.

Shy and reticent, Neumann was a 'Walter Mitty' who nevertheless translated his daydreams into action and adventure.

After having taken a Maasai spear through his forearm, seen his native servant carried off and eaten by a crocodile and been savaged by a cow elephant, Neumann made his hunting base in Samburu country where the Uaso Nyiro (Brown) River runs through landscape of jagged, forested moutains, dusty desert scrub and scorched grassland.

As in Neumann's day, seventy-five years ago, this is the kingdom of the stately Samburu ('Butterfly') people, brothers of the Maasai and like them conservative pastoralists living nomadic lives whose nursing mothers, old men and adolescents exist on a basic diet of cattle-blood, milk, and wild herbs.

With the exception of the eland antelope which they regard as 'wild cattle' (its roasted flesh does indeed taste like beef, and the animal is being commercially ranched in Kenya), the Maasai and Samburu do not kill animals for food. They measure their wealth in cattle.

The young Samburu, like the Maasai, wear black robes and lion's mane head-dresses as a prelude to circumcision ceremonies, then pass on to elaborately-styled hair-dos, bead necklaces and ivory earrings which they wear with dignity and vanity.

Unlike the wild animals, they are likely to get aggressive if a tourist declines to pay them a small fortune to pose for a photograph.

The Samburu Lodge at Neumann's camp site, 'Gateway to the North', is on a shady bank of the sandy river in some of the most excitingly unspoiled scenery in existence. It offers rest and relief — watching, for instance a family of elephant, trunk to tail, serenely crossing the stream — from the arid lands around, 200 miles from Nairobi.

Exotic animals, some of them quite different from those seen elsewhere in a land full of game, frequent this part of Kenya on the edge of the old Northern Frontier Province. Here lives the poacher-threatened Grevy's zebra, heavier than the common zebra, about a foot taller and with such thin stripes that from a distance the animal — named after President Grevy of France who was given one as a gift in 1881 by the King of Shoa in Ethiopia — appears to be pale grey. It is also recognised by its large, plate-shaped ears.

Cheetah and the pied wild dogs are more plentiful in Samburu than most other East African reserves, and it is the haven of dainty miniature antelopes known as dik-dik, fleeting shadows in the undergrowth; agile, bouncing impala, and the Beisa oryx with its long, rapier-sharp horns and reddish-grey coat. The tough skin of the Beisa bull's shoulder is prized by tribesmen for war-shields, and many a lion has lost a battle on the horns of this plucky animal.

A particularly weird inhabitant of the rugged terrain, where dead trees and sun-bleached bushes stand stark against a brazen sky, is the *aardvark*, or African ant-bear, that with its long, serpent's tongue robs termite hills at night. It is a frightening sight to meet at the full moon with its grotesque, red-brown body, kangaroo-tail, powerful claws, narrow head, rounded snout and long, pointed ears. It looks less like a bear than an apparition in a nightmare, but is harmless and makes a novel pet.

Red and yellow-billed hornbills, purple grenadiers, starlings with plumage like caskets of jewels, golden palm weavers, Nubian woodpeckers, white-bellied 'go away' birds and bou bou shrikes have become so tame that they will eat from the visitor's table or from his hand at the cedar-and-stone Samburu Lodge. It was built by a reformed big game hunter who hung up his high-velocity rifle and described himself as 'a former assassin'.

The broad, leafy river passes by the cupola lounge of Samburu Lodge, and in front of the open dining room so that at breakfast, lunch or dinner (from a menu that might feature fresh grilled trout) no game-viewing time is lost.

On the far bank, a leopard in the fork of a tree utters rapid, sawing grunts. Drinking elephant crowd a bend of the stream where herons and sacred ibis stand sentinel in the surging waters as malachite kingfishers flash past.

The grunting of lion, theme sound of all Africa, can be heard throughout the day and night.

The 'Crocodile Bar' of the lodge at river level allows Samburu's drinkers eye-to-eye confrontations with these armoured reptiles. They assemble on sandbanks below the lodge to bask like statues, jaws agape, in the sun. Snow-white egrets search their evil teeth for scraps of food. 'Danger, Crocodiles' reads a bold notice on the visitors' side of the bar. A board in view of the crocodiles on the riverside declares: 'Beware People'.

Overleaf: Eternal snow on Mt Kenya, a few miles from the Equator

View of Mount Kenya from Nyeri

Above: Giant groundsel (*Senecio johnstonii*), a characteristic plant
of the higher mountainous regions
Below: Cave waterfall in the Nyandarua Mountains
Left: Lewis glacier, Mount Kenya

'The Ark' Lodge in the Nyandarua 'Salient'

Group of buffalo

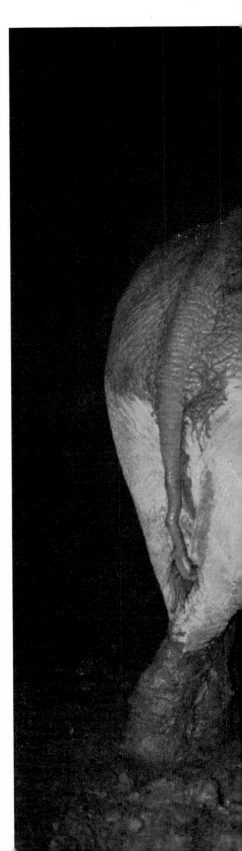

AT NIGHT AT 'THE ARK'

Far left: Bongo drinking
Left: Thick-tailed galago
Right: Genet on a balcony
Below left: Waterbuck
Below: Group of elephants

Chuka dancers

Meru huts in the Nyambeni Mountains

Meru girl carrying wood

Cheetah

Ostrich on the move

Elephants on the Uaso Nyiro River, Samburu
(also previous page)

Cheetah

Reticulated giraffe

Young serval cat

Rock hyrax

SAMBURU

Right: Grant's gazelle
Far right: Young Grevy's zebra
Below: Gerenuk feeding
Below right: Impala ram and females

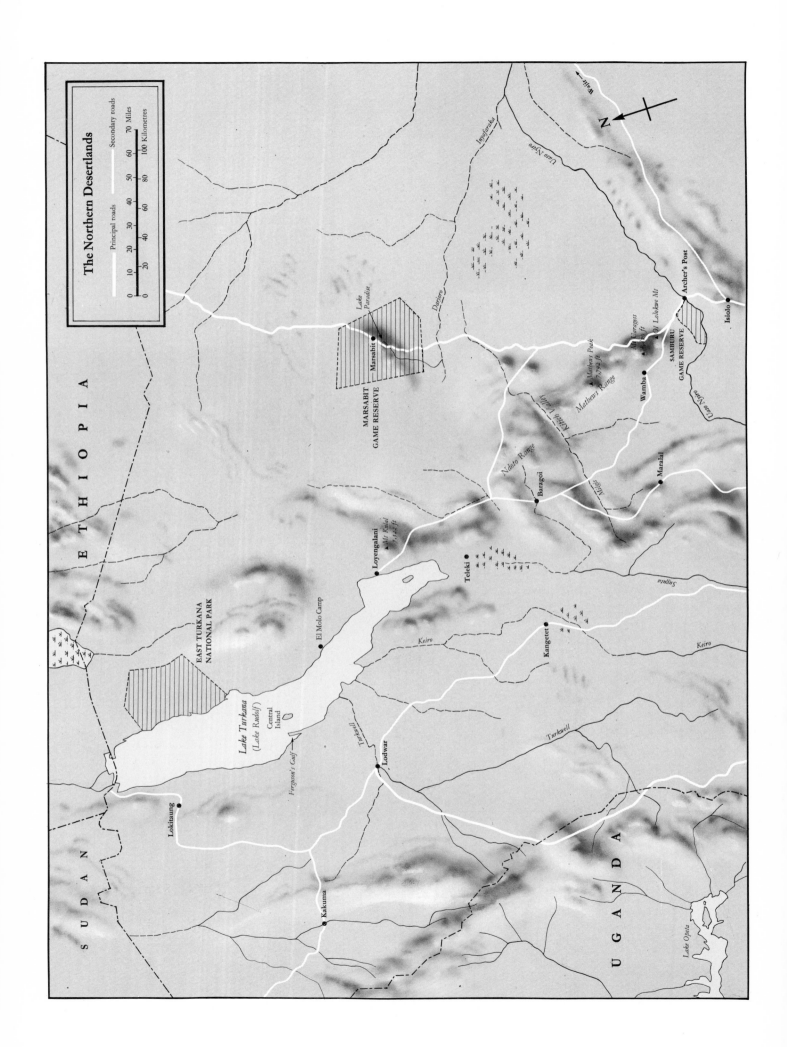

The Northern Desertlands

Principal roads
Secondary roads

70 Miles
100 Kilometres

N

ETHIOPIA

SUDAN

UGANDA

Lake Turkana
(Lake Rudolf)

Central Island

Ferguson's Gulf

EAST TURKANA
NATIONAL PARK

El Molo Camp

Loyengalani

Mt. Kulal
8,122 ft

Teleki

Lokitaung

Lodwar

Turkwell

Turkwell

Kakuma

Lake Opeta

Kangetet

Keiro

Keiro

Suguta

Baragoi

Ndoto Range

Nyiro

Marsabit

MARSABIT
GAME RESERVE

Lake
Paradise

Darimo

Ngularaka

Uaso Nyiro

Archer's Post

Isiolo

SAMBURU
GAME RESERVE

Ol Lolokwe Mt.

Mt. Uragess
8,640 ft

Mathews Peak
7,792 ft

Mathews Range

Kirisia Hills

Wamba

Maralal

Wait

4

Desertlands

Straggling, dusty Isiolo in northern Kenya is the meeting place of many different cultures, of peoples and creeds, camels and cattle, highland and scrub desert, and of the Nilo-Hamite, Bantu and Hamite.

Leaving the town, the scenes become Biblical. There is the trail of pack camels through arid country. Donkeys and their Semitic drivers trudge across brazen sand to their trading stations. Waterholes are surrounded by emaciated goats, camels and cattle.

The 'signpost' to the far north is the dramatically spectacular Ol Lolokwe Mountain. Its huge cliff, facing the main road out of Isiolo, reflects superb colourings at different times of the day, especially in the early morning and late afternoon.

For those who love the genuinely wild, the remote and unspoilt, northern Kenya is one of the most memorable and exciting places in existence.

On a trek up to the 'Jade Sea' of Lake Turkana (formerly Rudolf), following old camel tracks, some of the more adventurous with time on their hands might care to make a detour to Wajir in the east. It's worth it — if only for a chuckle at the recent past. Wajir is a Beau Geste-style desert outpost complete with 'Foreign Legion' fort, palm oasis, and scores of camels. Although there is not a drop of sailing water anywhere around, it is the site of the 'Royal Wajir Yacht Club'.

Many years ago the small, white colonial staff, whose *askaris* guarded the only well there from sepia-skinned bandits, built a shanty pub in the shape of a ship. With British humour, they named it 'The Wajir Yacht Club'. Mess dress was a black bow tie and a *kikoi*, or wrap-around skirt: and the few people who came through Wajir were made honorary members if they passed the committee's tests. For instance, they might be required to climb a greasy pole (naked except for the bow tie), drink a gallon of beer at a sitting, or sing an aria from *La Bohème*.

When the late Duke of Windsor, then Prince of Wales, visited the slightly dotty colonial exiles at Wajir during an African tour, he was spared any public ordeal as his 'dues' for membership. In return for the club's hospitality he gave it a royal charter.

Short on membership and upkeep since Kenya's independence, the Royal Wajir Yacht Club is now used as a resthouse by the local Camel Corps, between forays against *shifta* (bandits) and livestock rustlers. Only ghostly laughter disturbs their sleep.

Back on the rocky northern road, Uaraguess, at 8,820 ft. the principal mountain of the Mathews Range, comes slowly into view like a photographic print being developed.

Uaraguess is covered to its summit with forests that were once alive with elephant, rhino, and Colobus monkeys. From the summit, consisting of three massive rock buttresses, the climber looks down on martial eagles with eight foot wingspans wheeling in the mists far below.

West of Uaraguess, the rest of the Mathews Range (named after an old-time British general who was in charge of the sultan's army in Zanzibar) have great rain forests at their peaks, and these have produced an important river at Kitich, 75 miles north of Archer's Post. In a valley of the Kitich, the maneless desert lion is likely to be encountered in Kenya for the first time.

Even more splendid than the Mathews are the peaks of the Ndoto Range close by.

Lying south of Lake Turkana is Marsabit, the most remote of the country's major game parks (350 miles from Nairobi), a visit being still something of an exploit yielding rich returns. A refreshingly green massif rising out of the desert wilderness, littered with black lava, the reserve takes its name from this 5,593 ft. volcanic mountain, heavily forested, that is the home of the elephants who carry some of the heaviest and most beautiful ivory in Africa – possibly because of nutritive minerals in the soil.

Here roamed 'Ahmed', the long-tusked bull elephant who, under presidential protection, became the symbol of wildlife conservation in Kenya and a living national monument until he died of old age a few years ago.

Marsabit elephant, the park's chief attraction, still have tusks of 100 lb. or more, and there are one or two up and coming contenders for Ahmed's title of 'King of the African Elephants'.

The lodge in Marsabit National Park is built on the edge of a lush volcanic crater, providing a natural vantage point to view the game. Reticulated giraffe, elephant, the regal, helter-skelter-horned Greater kudu, lion, leopard and striped hyena emerge from the forest to feed and drink on the crater floor.

The sheer cliffs of Marsabit Mountain are the eyries of the rare lammergeyer.

Marsabit is an important gathering place for nomadic tribesmen – the Boran, Rendile, Gabra and Somalis – who bring their camels and livestock in from the desert and draw water to rhythmic chanting at the district's 'Singing Wells'.

The Boran, whose territory extends into Ethiopia, possess short-horned cattle around whom their lives revolve. Many Boran are Moslems, but among the pagans of the tribe there are snake-worshippers and young men who must have killed a fellow human or a fierce animal in order to be initiated into manhood. A caravan of Boran, with their flowing white robes and hawk-like features, is a print taken from the Old Testament.

The Gabra too are wide-ranging, cattle-herding nomads.

The Rendile, naked above the waist except for necklaces and other bead ornaments, carry portable shelters of hides and poles like furled black sails on the backs of their camels. The animals' lurching gait sets the flat wooden bells round their necks tolling.

Proud and quick-tempered, the Somalis are tall with narrow, handsome features. The men wear a long, white cloth like a Roman toga, and invariably carry a dagger. The younger women are stately and beautiful, their dark hair dressed with herb-scented oils.

Besides its wildlife and photo-album tribespeople, the Marsabit region has some imposing lakes when the volcanic craters fill with water after the rains. The best-known is circular Lake Paradise, surrounded by an emerald marsh. It was visited by the Queen Mother before she became Queen Elizabeth, and was for four years the home of Martin and Olga Johnson, the Americans who pioneered wildlife adventure films in the twenties.

More than thirty years earlier – in March 1888 – explorers Samuel Teleki von Szek, a count of the Holy Roman Empire, and his Austrian companion, Lieutenant Ludwig von Höhnel (later an admiral), had discovered a great wonderland of water away to the north-west of Marsabit.

Von Höhnel wrote of their arrival at Loyengalani at the south-eastern end of the lake: 'We hurried as fast as we could to the top of our ridge, the scene gradually developing itself as we advanced, until an entirely new world was spread before our astonished eyes. The void down in the depths beneath became filled as if by magic with picturesque mountains and rugged slopes, with a medley of ravines and valleys, which appeared to be closing up from every side to form a fitting frame for the dark-blue gleaming surface of the lake stretching away beyond as far as the eye could reach.

'For a long time we gazed in speechless delight, spell-bound by the beauty of the scene before us, whilst our men, equally silent, stared into the distance for a few minutes: to break presently into shouts of astonishment at the sight of the glittering expanse of the great lake which melted on the horizon into the blue of the sky. At that moment all our dangers, all our fatigues were forgotten in the joy of finding our exploring crowned with success at last.'

By then the members of the expedition were haggard from exhaustion, and suffering raging thirsts. The sheet of water before them – 'set like a pearl of great price in the wonderful landscape beneath us' – promised instant relief and they scrambled down a sharp, lava escarpment to the lake.

It was a cruel experience.

'The beautiful water stretched away before us, clear as crystal. The men rushed down shouting, but soon returned in bitter disappointment. The water was brackish. What a betrayal!'

Count Teleki and von Höhnel named the vast stretch of water, 'Rudolf' after their sponsor and patron, Prince Rudolf, Archduke and Crown Prince of Austria, who in a famous tragedy at Mayerling a year later murdered his lovely young mistress and committed suicide.

Teleki's dormant volcano still stands on the southern shore, but President Kenyatta changed the name of the lake to 'Turkana' after the nomadic people of that name.

At Loyengalani, on sandy islands and the barren, blistering hot beach of a bay, Teleki and von Höhnel encountered a tiny Stone Age tribe, the fish-eating El Molo. In local dialect, this simply means, with every justification, 'Poor devils'.

Von Höhnel describes the El Molo as living 'upon two unimportant and perfectly barren sandbanks rising but little above the level of the lake', adding: 'The two islands together are not more than half or one square mile in extent. On the larger are from thirty to fifty, and on the smaller about fifteen, brown huts, of hayrick shape, huddled closely together.'

He found other small groups of El Molo on the mainland shore opposite these sandbanks.

'There are about 200 or 300 Elmolo [sic] altogether, and they support themselves by fishing, which must be very fruitful of results, for though they neither cultivate cereals nor obtain them by barter, they did not look as if they suffered from scanty diet. They were ignorant of the use of tobacco.

'The hair is dressed in various fashions, either dragged up into a short, thin tuft which is thickly smeared with red fat, or combed back flat, and, with the help of some greasy green or violet-coloured clay, moulded into quite an artistic-looking chignon. The latter style is peculiar to young men, and is sometimes finished off with two short ostrich feathers. When touched, this chignon will be found to have a thin hardened outer layer of clay, whilst the inside is quite soft, like a pad. Rings are worn in the lobe and sides of the ear, but the lobes are very slightly distended. Other ornaments are bracelets worn on the upper and the lower arm, made of brass or iron wire or of hippopotamus hide. A round knife is also sometimes worn as a bracelet, the edges being protected.

'The very simple costume of the men consists merely of a circular apron about two and a half inches long in front and six inches long behind, made of dressed kid-skin, the edges of which are very prettily decorated with a row of gleaming home-made iron beads. The rounded knives already mentioned, bows, arrows, and some inferior spears complete their equipment. I must add that all the men, but none of the women, carry a little stool to sit upon, which also serves them as a pillow at night.'

Since von Höhnel's writings, the emaciated and rickets-deformed El Molo, ranking alongside the Bushmen of the Kalahari desert as one of the smallest and most primitive tribes ever known in Africa, have been fighting their way back from the brink of extinction.

At one time, these strange people whose exact origins are unknown (they believe they are descended from fish) were down to 75 men, women and children. Scientists in the early seventies believed they were doomed.

Their recovery against fearful odds – today their body count is around 300 and they seem out of danger of oblivion – is little short of a miracle.

The bow-legged El Molo very rarely ate meat – and then only hippo – and never milk or vegetables. Not a blade of grass grows in the furnace-like heat of their rocky wasteland, and the burning sun heats the ground to a temperature at which little or no plant life can survive. Their rough, dome-style huts of reeds, driftwood, thorn bushes and doum palm leaves scattered on the harsh shores are lashed by scorching blasts of wind off the lake of up to a hundred miles an hour. Boulders and stones are used to hold down these pitiful 'homes'.

The puny El Molo women in braided skirts or palm fibres hardly had the strength to bear children or to cook over the goat-dung fires the fish the men in tattered loin-cloths harpooned from log-rafts. The lock of a dead elder's hair that the El Molo tribesman carries inside his mud-bun hair-do to give him muscle and protection seemed to be no guarantee against a slow and miserable death from chronic malnutrition.

Then one day the El Molo had an inspiration. They pooled their skinny goats as the *lobola*, or bride price, for a buxom girl from the neighbouring Samburu tribe.

Given into marriage with one of the more vigorous El Molo youths, she helped increase the 'Fish People's' numbers. Other such marriages, followed. As, incredibly, the El Molo believed they already possessed all nature could provide and stubbornly refused to leave their barren homeland for more congenial parts down south, the Kenya government decided a few years ago to establish a viable fishing industry on Lake Turkana and to supply them with maize, dried milk, food concentrates, boats and fishing tackle.

The government and Catholic priests and nuns are co-operating in providing mission hospitals, medical care and educational facilities for the El Molo who have broken down tribal barriers to increase their numbers with new blood. For better or for worse, the re-born tribe will not abandon the fishing skills (in a lake, teeming with crocodiles and hippo) that they have acquired since time immemorial. For there is no assurance that they can survive without fish, the staple food.

Hippo meat forms a very small part of the El Molo's monotonous diet; sandals are made from the hide. A hippopotamus hunt by young El Molo has the same social significance as a lion-killing ceremony once held for the Maasai *moran*. A young man sets out to kill a two-ton hippo single-handed by spearing it in the water and pulling on ropes attached to the spears until the victim dies. He is then felt to have demonstrated his bravery, and his fitness for a monogamous marriage in accordance with the old law of the tribe.

Barren Loyengalani, which ironically means 'The Place of the Trees' (although it *does* have a swimming pool fed by a spring), has become a base for bird-watching expeditions by boat to South Island.

Fishing trips are run from Loyengalani for the rare golden perch and the Nile perch which are often longer and heavier than the angler. They will take a tennis shoe used as a lure and are the largest freshwater fish alive. The record Lake Turkana perch weighed 375 lbs.

As a result of their recent contact with tourist parties at Loyengalani, El Molo women have acquired a taste for both chewing gum and tobacco. They do not enjoy smoking cigarettes given to them, but grind the tobacco between pebbles to make snuff which they carry around in little clay pots.

In 1970, a thousand square miles of the eastern shore and rugged hinterland of the lake was set aside as 'a recreation area' and a national park for the protection of wildlife, including the crocodile and hippo populations and such northern game species as oryx, topi and small antelope. The game guards pack rifles and ride camels.

The reserve is undeveloped and without the circuit tracks and lodges of older, more sophisticated animal preserves, but camping is possible with the permission of the warden.

East Turkana National Park is ideal for anyone determined to get away from it all, to relax and enjoy himself amid a lonely scene of land and water painted in startling, primary colours.

From March to early May, the lake and its 'Martian' surrounds are the landing grounds of great numbers of migrant wildfowl from Europe, also wagtails and marsh sandpipers. There are many thousands of flamingo on Turkana, as well as gulls, egrets, ibis, waders, pelicans, ducks and geese.

Prince Philip, a dedicated conservationist, has been one of many enthusiastic bird-watchers there, training his binoculars on such rarities as the black-tailed godwit and the spotted redshank. Far from jostling crowds and the cares and responsibilities of royal office, Prince Philip told his aides during his idyllic Lake Turkana sojourn that it was one of the happiest times of his life.

Three rivers flow into greenish-blue Lake Turkana, once a source of the Nile, but curiously none flow out. Covering 3,500 square miles at an altitude of 1,200 ft., the lake is estimated to contain at least 25,000 crocodiles whose underbelly skins are covered in warts and therefore generally unsuitable for women's handbags and shoes.

The lake, 150 miles long and averaging about 20 miles wide, ringed by red hills streaked with green and white and weird stretches of purple lava, is mildly alkaline. Its abundant aquatic life includes large shoals of the fierce tigerfish, considered among the finest sporting fish in the register, and *tilapia* that are best eaten after being smoked over smouldering grasses. The crocodiles feed so well off fish that they rarely bother to attack human beings.

Lake Turkana is often struck by fierce storms that seem to originate, without warning, from its south-eastern tip, the site of Mount Kulal, Teleki's heavily-eroded conical volcano. When Vivian Fuchs, conqueror of Antarctica, visited South Island in the thirties two members of his party were drowned after a vicious squall wrecked their boat.

The stark north-eastern shores have been combed by palaeontological expeditions headed by Richard Leakey, whose camp at Koobi Fora has been the base of his immensely productive search for the origins of man.

On the western shore, there is a most attractive fishing camp at Ferguson's Gulf. Many tourists come here from Nairobi in the hope of returning home with a fishing story to end all fishing stories.

Ferguson's Gulf is also the place from which to visit Central Island with its steep-walled volcanic craters and crater lakes that are the haunt of elegant flamingo.

Barely influenced by the outside world are the Turkana, a proud cattle people after whom the lake has been given its modern, 'Africanised' name. Being of the 'Karamojong Cluster', as the tribes are called, the Turkana have relatives in Uganda and the southern Sudan. They occupy the whole of the arid north-western corner of Kenya, with its centre at Lodwar.

Strong individualists, like all the pastoral Nile Hamites they are a vain and striking people. They continue to live in a traditional style, far removed from trends of the age, that is ideally suited to their remote and arid existence among the sand-dunes. The men have elaborate hair styles, fashioned from clay and dung, that are overhauled every two or three months and are usually dyed blue. Eagle feathers and a curved reed add a final touch to this coiffure. Like the El Molo of von Höhnel's day, they carry a small, wooden neck-stool, hung from the wrist, which they use as a pillow at night to protect their crowning glory.

Besides their formidable hunting spear, the warriors carry a knife with a handle that encircles the wrist, together with other deadly symbols of manhood. On ceremonial occasions, the men put on leopard skin capes and ostrich feather head-dresses.

Both men and women wear earrings and lip-plugs to which the women, who enjoy a high status unlike the females of other tribes, add lavish bead ornaments and necklaces of ostrich egg-shell worked into small discs. Leather aprons still commonly worn by the Turkana women and girls are decorated with vagina-shaped cowrie shells from the coast, the ancient Kenyan symbols of fertility. For all that, the Turkana have a series of initiation ceremonies during which two teeth are removed from the lower jaw — as a sign of beauty.

They have large numbers of camels, and mixed herds of cattle, sheep and goats. Their main nourishment is milk from the animals, principally the camel. These beasts will give two or three times as much milk as a cow when there is some scrub pasture to be found. They will continue to give milk during a drought when the cow had dried up. Like the Rendile, the Turkana travel with their own villages — loading shelters of skins and poles on to camels and donkeys before they go off on their wanderings. While the men move around for weeks with the herds, the older women may remain behind at some semi-permanent location to grow crops by a deep waterhole they have dug with crude tools in a dry river-bed.

The Turkana's pack-camels are hired for a hardy, new form of holiday adventure that is proving popular in the lava-strewn regions of the moody but magnificent lake. Prince Charles pioneered one of these — a week long 'camel safari' that began outside Isiolo and made its way north through the mission station of Wamba.

Overleaf: Seyia Luga with the Mathews Range foothills

Camel trek along the Seyia luga

Loading up

Boran at Marsabit

Somali cattle in the Magado crater, between Isiolo and
Garba Tula

Boran

Gabra

Preparing a camel saddle

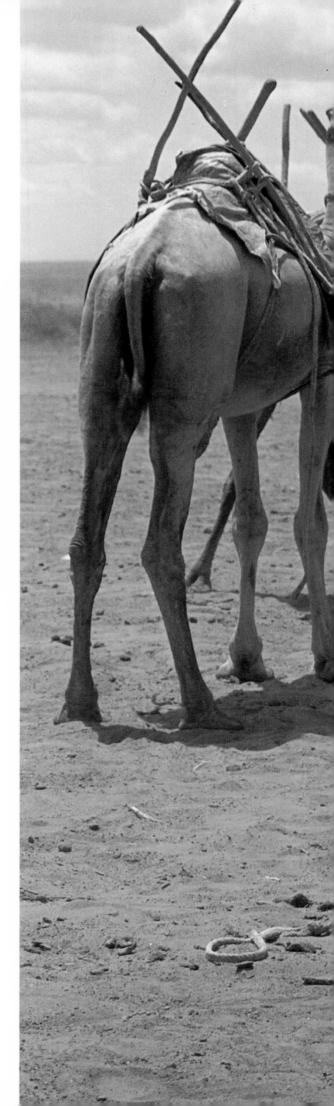

Gabra girl and camels

Ndoto Mountains

Olowa Werikoi Mountain near Wamba

View towards Mount Porr and Lake Turkana from Loyengalani

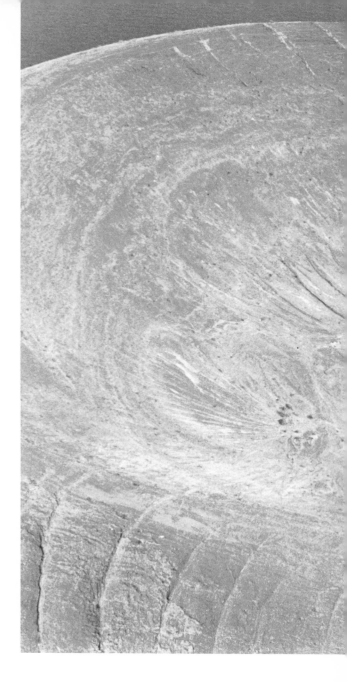

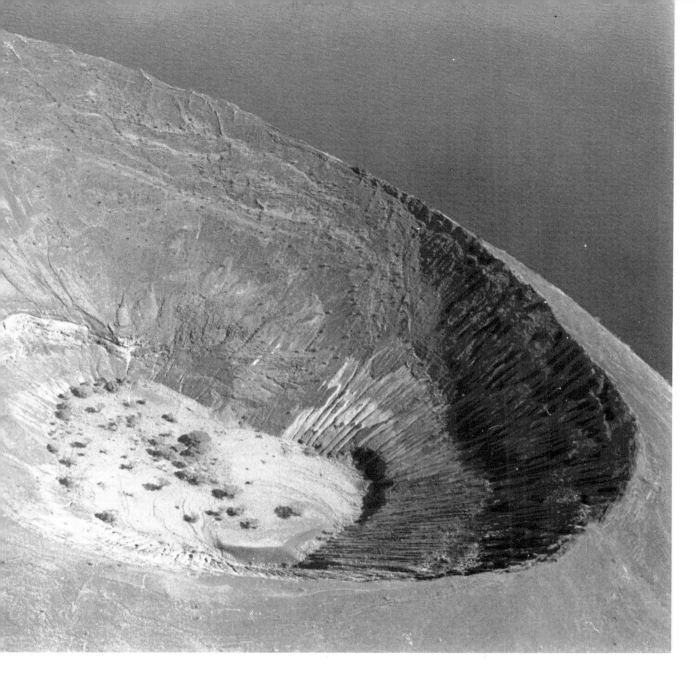

Extinct volcanic crater at the southern end of Lake Turkana

El Molo camp near Loyengalani, Lake Turkana

Turkana boys beside Lake Turkana

Turkana woman, senior wife of a manyatta headman

Turkana herdsboy and cattle

Pregnant Samburu woman

Left: Male Agama lizard
(*Agama agama*)
Dung beetle at work
Termite mounds
Below: Vulturine guinea-fowl
Right: Chameleon
Far right: Cistanche tubulosa
Right below: Adenium obesum

Turkana woman milking goat

Turkana woman feeding child in her manyatta

Pokot gold-panning in the Morun River

Samburu woman

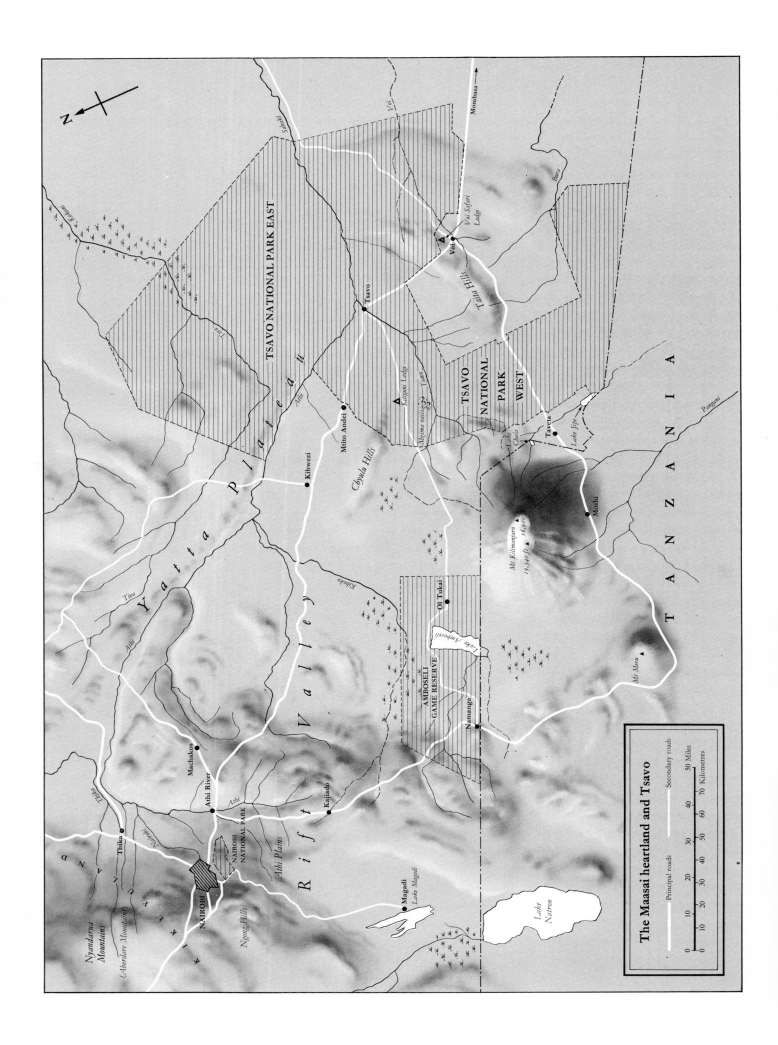

Z

Nyandarua
Mountains

Aberdare Mountains

Thika

Thika

Tana

Nairobi

NAIROBI

Ngong Hills

KIKUYULAND

Machakos

Athi River

Athi

NAIROBI
NATIONAL
PARK

Athi Plains

Magadi

Lake Magadi

Kajiado

Athi

Tiva

Athi

Y a t t a   P l a t e a u

R i f t   V a l l e y

Kolomu

Tiva

Athi

Tiva

Sabaki

TSAVO NATIONAL PARK EAST

Kibwezi

Mtito Andei

Cbyulu Hills

Kiboko

AMBOSELI
GAME RESERVE

Ol Tukai

Lake Amboseli

Namanga

Lake Natron

Tsavo

Voi

Kilaguni Lodge

Mzima oasis

Tyapo

TSAVO
NATIONAL
PARK   WEST

Lake Chala

Taveta

Lake Jipe

Mt Kilimanjaro
19,340 ft
16,900

Moshi

Mt Meru

Taita Hills

Voi

Voi Safari
Lodge

Mombasa

Bura

Pangani

T A N Z A N I A

The Maasai heartland and Tsavo

——— Principal roads   ——— Secondary roads

0   10   20   30   40   50 Miles
0   20   30   40   50   60   70 Kilometres

5

The Maasai Heartland and Tsavo

A Maasai fable tells how the dying white-haired Great Chief Le-Eyo called his children around him to take leave of them and distribute his wealth.

Asked what he wanted, the eldest son replied: 'Something of everything on earth'.

Le-Eyo shook his head sadly.

'Then take a few head of cattle, some goats and sheep and some food of the earth', he said.

The younger son, however, asked only for a fly-whisk made from the tail hairs of a giraffe that the old man carried.

'My child', said his father, 'God will give you wealth because you have chosen only this. You will be great among your brother's people'.

The fable relates how the greedy elder son became a barbarian while the younger brother who spurned riches and material comforts grew up to become the father of Kenya's noble warrior tribe: the Maasai.

At one time they dominated most of the other East African tribes, having standing armies drawn from youthful age-grades who went into battle with bravery, resource and skills matched only by the fierce *impis* of the Zulus down south.

Since then they have rubbed shoulders with Hollywood film stars. Ernest Hemingway applauded the handsome, teenage warriors leaping stiffly four feet in the air in a ritual dance of manhood, their oily, plaited hair streaming out behind them.

They have been photographed a million times by tourists — the tribesmen smearing red ochre and grey mud over each other's tall, stately bodies; the women smirking shyly in deep necklets of rainbow-coloured beads, or families drinking clotted ox-blood, mixed with wild herbs and curdled milk, from a gourd. Old tribal laws decree they shall not kill their cattle — their wealth — for meat.

Now the spectacle of the haughty, marathon-loping Maasai on the undulating plains of Kenya is rapidly fading. It is being replaced, due to official persuasion, with modern models of Africa's statuesque pastoralists, no longer dressed merely in a thin, ragged cloth but proudly astride a tractor in khaki shorts; in the bush-shirt, trousers and snake-boots of game wardens; wearing a smartly-cut western suit as a Government Minister, or in a senior policeman's uniform.

The Maasai tribesmen and their families are being wooed by posters and propaganda campaigns from the nomadic life to game conservation, settled farming, veterinary courses, adult literacy centres, homecraft classes and general nation-building projects like the construction of roads, schools and clinics.

Governmental efforts — now bearing fruit — have long been directed at getting Maasai factions to settle down and not wander the countryside with hundreds of thousands of domestic beasts, creating dead lands and depriving the wild animals of their habitats.

I have a long-standing Maasai friend who was born in a dark, fly-ridden mud hut and today holds a Bachelor of Arts degree. He was once a herdboy roaming the hills with steers, cows and calves. Like many other Maasai youngsters, he could 'talk' to lions in a series of deep-throated grunts and beguiling whines — to which, as I have seen and heard, they respond with cocked ears, heads to one side and rumblings that could be entire sentences. Today, this tri-lingual Maasai, for he can also speak English and Swahili fluently, sits behind a desk in government service.

'I belonged to two worlds even at a fairly early age', he says. 'I was in a Christian school with a Christian name, yet I had to take part in the Maasai rites for boys.

'As part of a group, I was given a symbolic father. During the holidays, I had to strip off my school clothes and go off alone into the bush. It was part of an early toughening-up process.

'The young initiate has to sleep out in the open among dangerous wild animals. He has to be able to defend himself, without a weapon of any sort, against a lion or a charging rhino, if necessary.

'Before you apply to the "father" of your group to become a *moran*, or warrior, you must be able to show him you are able to take the place of the outgoing *moran* who is to pass into a new phase of the tribal structure.

'While these youngsters are segregated and brought up under a strict code of discipline, they had a good, carefree life with plenty of girl friends — although they are not expected to eat any food touched by a women — and were generally not keen to give it up. So you have to battle, literally. You have to be able to fight a *moran*, with stout staves as weapons, and win. There's nothing gentle like punching. Maasai boys are not allowed to punch. Only the girls can use their fists. You must demonstrate your courage in every possible way until all in your age group have proved they are ready for the next step.

'This is the circumcision ceremony. Under the knife, you must not give the slightest sign of fear or pain — not blink an eyelid or flinch throughout the whole operation. And beforehand you are constantly and deliberately insulted by others of the tribe who yell "coward", and worse, and try to make you crack up before the actual suffering ahead.

'Well, our battle groups once struck terror into tribesmen throughout East Africa, and I suppose this sort of commando training was necessary then.'

But the circumcision operation, that crude test of fortitude, did not in itself make the youth a warrior. It is, however, the last stage before the ceremony of becoming a *moran*. The initiate is not required — for the government has long banned the practice — to seek out a male lion and slay the creature single-handed with a long-bladed war spear as the ultimate test of his manhood.

'The day I became a warrior in the records of the Maasai, I was washed and shaved from head to foot. All my clothing was thrown away, and I was given a new Maasai name. You have to lose everything you can of your previous existence.

'I did not have to wear the customary two black ostrich feathers in my hair, blackened cloth, chalk all over my body and those white facial patterns that

134

define a warrior-to-be. But, with the others due to become fighting men, I was fed the blood of cattle mixed with milk – a lot of milk and very little blood, thank goodness. I did not like it much. The mixture was at one time given to a *moran* wounded in battle as a form of transfusion and is by no means as widely used by the Maasai as is generally believed, particularly now. Some of the women who have to drink it to help recovery after childbirth can only bring themselves to swallow it in the dark.'

One of the dying rites of the Maasai is the *ewunoto* ceremony, wild and semi-secret, that used to take place every seven years. Marking the creation of a new generation of junior elders, the *ewunoto* represents the 'cleansing' phase at the end of a series of ceremonies designed to ensure the young Maasai will become a loyal and hard-working member of the tribe.

At one of the performances of this rite I was allowed to watch, thousands of Maasai men, women and children gathered in a clearing in the bush and squatted in a huge circle as the youthful *morani* (warriors) stamped out their dances as spearmen guardians of the tribe. They went through the shadow-play of slaying a lion. Behind a screen of tall bushes, headmen tied cow-hide thongs round the middle fingers of the initiates whose nude bodies, ghostly in white ash, were decorated with elaborate designs.

Finally, the new young leaders snaked down into the arena from a wind-swept escarpment. Wearing devil masks of mahogany, head-dresses of black and white eagles' feathers and with their crimson capes billowing like flames around them, the leaping and prancing youngsters chanted for five hours war songs of a bygone age. At sundown, they collapsed to the pock-marked red earth and the ceremony was at an end.

Nothing is being done at governmental level to perpetuate the *ewunoto* and other tribal rituals as the Maasai – no longer merely 'museum pieces' on display for tourists – move with ever-lengthening strides into the 20th century. At Kajiado, the administrative centre of the tribe on the Athi Plain en route to Amboseli, they are learning that the pen is mightier than the spear taking courses in animal husbandry and wildlife management.

'My people were once great hunters of the lion, the elephant and the rhino', said a grizzled Maasai chief there. 'These animals were our enemies. Today they are our friends.

'We have long realised the value of preserving them because the money from tourists who come from all over the world has helped us to become good and useful citizens.'

The Maasai claim that their 700 square mile Mara Reserve in south-western Kenya shelters more wildlife than any area of comparable size in the world. Established as a sanctuary in 1961, it is acknowledged by many others besides the Maasai to be the best of all Kenya's animal reserves.

Some tourists fly there, but the more intrepid who go by road are rewarded by a pioneering sense of adventure and some spectacular scenery. After skirting the volcano of Longonot and a satellite communications station, the road passes through the small township of Narok crossing miles and miles of plains dotted with game. Suddenly an oasis of thorn trees signals the presence of the Mara River. This, as the American writer Robert Ruark described it, is 'Hollywood Africa'.

A popular terrain for photo-safaris, Prince Charles camped in the Maasai Mara in 1971. The incredible abundance of game there takes the visitor back to the dawn of man's history. Herds of Cape buffalo, zebra, the blue-shanked topi, the rare roan antelope, wildebeest, giraffe and gazelles roam the rolling grasslands. There are thick, shady forests along rivers full of hippo and crocodiles. Prides of lion up to 30 in number are found among the tall grasses of the savannah, some of the males black-maned; and there are relatively bountiful populations of elephant, cheetah and leopard.

At one of the Mara's new tourist lodges, the guests lost their early morning tea when a waiter came face to face with a lion, dropped his tray and fled.

Although cut off by the Great Sand River, the Maasai Mara is really an extension of neighbouring Tanzania's Serengeti National Park and shares to some degree the annual migration of millions of wildebeest and zebra in search of adequate drinking water and grazing. The young, the weak and the old, die in their thousands from drowning, diseases, or the onslaughts of lions and other predators as the animals, a seething black mass, fill the landscape of plains and rivers on this fabulous yearly trek.

Unlike some other animal reserves in Kenya, drivers are not confined to tracks in the Mara and can go 'bundu-bashing', or bushwhacking. Tourists based at Keekorok Lodge or tented camps are taken out on foot safaris by a Maasai guide who carries not a gun but a long-bladed spear as protection against wild animals.

The Mara claims to have the best game-viewing operation in existence — history's first and only regular hot-air balloon service. It costs £60 or so an hour, and visitors almost queue up to pay the fee.

European balloon pilots have obtained a concession from the Maasai to operate a service that provides a thrilling new dimension to wildlife watching and game photography. The original orange-and-yellow balloon among those used, is 60 ft. wide, the height of a ten storey building and named 'Lengai' after a Maasai god who lives in the fires of a local active volcano.

The dreamlike rides begin at a calm dawn each day for three, or a maximum of four, passengers whose ages may range from eight to eighty. One of the intrepid balloonists (they are given ornate certificates for their 'courage and faith', at the end of each flight) wrote this lyrical description of the start of his trip:

> Suddenly the petrol-driven fan clatters into life and the engine roar proclaims a more urgent rhythm to the morning stillness. Trained hands hold open the mouth of the balloon and the fan inflates the limp fabric which grows slowly into a slug — a bubble — a tent — a monstrous, swelling whale — and finally a glorious cathedral of vibrant golden cloth.
>
> Lying on its side, the balloon is suddenly and unbelievably enormous with almost a life of its own, gaping mouth waiting to drink the roaring flames of gas from the big burners.
>
> John (the pilot) shoots the twenty-foot jets of fire into the belly of the balloon which quivers, awakes and stands up with ponderous dignity.
>
> Now the balloon holds many tons of air.
>
> In a few moments of quiet hurry, passengers climb into the basket, an empty cylinder is discarded, cameras are checked and then another tiny squirt of flame overcomes the equilibrium; the balloon, basket and passengers move gently upwards, one moment intimately connected with onlookers who pass sunglasses and binoculars into the basket, the next moment departed as irrevocably as passengers on the rail of a liner slipping slowly and imperceptibly from the quay.
>
> Now, in the basket, it is a magic world as the ground drops silently away and the vistas open over the trees. Floating free on the wind, the

balloon drifts over the rolling Mara Hills giving sometimes a bird's eye view and sometimes a close-up of the wildlife, for the balloon can come down within inches of the ground only to be raised aloft once more by skilful application of the burners.

Having risen like a bubble of air through water, the balloon hangs as a psychedelic tear in a blue sky flecked with the crimson shafts of dawn. All around, stretching to hazy infinity, is raw Africa. It takes a minute or two to adjust to this lighter-than-air flight with no wings, no engines, no propellers, no sensation of vertigo or turbulence, nor (when the burners are turned off) any sound but the creaking of the gently swaying wicker basket.

The olive-green Mara landscape contrasts starkly with the black shadow of the balloon as it drifts a few hundred feet above a score of unsuspecting elephant. A lioness is seen stalking a young antelope as a long trail of bearded gnus surge round the 'hillock' of a lone rhino in their path.

An inquisitive, scrawny-necked vulture floats alongside, stately and graceful in flight yet so repugnant when feeding on the remain's of a big cat's kill.

Seen clearly from the on-a-cloud viewpoint of the balloon's basket, a leopard breaks cover from a rocky outcrop and leaps into the thorny branches of an acacia tree.

On the horizon, villages of box-like Maasai huts fashioned from river mud are wreathed in smoke and gilded by shafts of sunlight.

Landings, smooth or bumpy, are followed by a champagne breakfast at the spot where a recovery team packs the balloon into a safari truck. Passengers are invited to write their comments in the balloon's log. Typical entries are: 'I felt like a butterfly'; 'Game-viewing from a minibus will never be the same again'; 'You can have the Jumbo jets'; 'A childhood fantasy come true'; and 'I have found a special serenity'.

Kenya's border with Tanzania stretches south-eastwards in a straight line from the Mara to Mount Kilimanjaro, cutting through the Rift Valley south of Lake Magadi.

The lake is 30 miles long but contains only ten feet of water at its deepest point. In a dusty depression, it is surrounded by shimmering soda pans, some crystalline white, others rose-pink, matching the countless flamingoes searching for algae round the shores. The concentration of soda in Lake Magadi is so heavy that some years ago a rescue operation had to be mounted by game wardens to save hundreds of flamingo chicks whose spindly legs had become encrusted with heavy anklets of salt. They were unable to fly with their parents.

Each year Magadi provides hundreds of thousands of tons of commercial soda-ash, used both in common salt and for making glass, for home and export markets.

In this torrid, tinder-dry part of the Rift, evaporation greatly exceeds rainfall and so Magadi is almost solid soda, or trona — combinations of sodium carbonates. Magadi has the second largest deposit of trona in the world, after the Salton Sea in California, and provides one of Kenya's most valuable mineral resources. The Magadi trona regenerates almost as fast as it is removed for commercial purposes.

Lake Magadi has no outlet, but contains a few million years' worth of alkaline brines derived from springs from the Rift Valley's soda-rich volcanic rocks. The lake gives off a pungent odour, and its fish—*tilapia*—that live in and around its hot springs die if put in cold water. It is the only known breeding ground in Kenya of the avocet, a dainty black-and-white plover with blue-grey legs that feeds on water insects among the salt pans with a scything motion of its thin, upturned bill.

Unattractive Magadi town, one of the hottest and driest places in Kenya, boasts a golf course. But its 'greens' (taken over now and then by a giraffe or a warthog) are made of black earth.

Handed over to Maasai trusteeship shortly before Kenya's independence, Amboseli Game Sanctuary at the foot of majestic Mount Kilimanjaro is ancient Africa in microcosm.

The mountain that is the world's fourth highest volcano, surpassed only by three in the Andes, was once part of what is now the Republic of Kenya.

In 1886 a joint commission drew up a boundary in East Africa between British and German spheres of influence, but Kaiser Wilhelm complained to his aunt, Queen Victoria, that this would give her two 'snow-capped mountains', Kilimanjaro and Mount Kenya, and him none. It was therefore agreed— in such an arbitrary and childish fashion were some colonial borders laid down — that the Kenya boundary should skirt the base of mighty Kilimanjaro so that Wilhelm and Victoria could have one snowy mountain each.

Amboseli, where the mountain 'floats' like a cloud-ringed mirage in the sky, was once an area used for hunting safaris and is the setting for Hemingway's *The Snows of Kilimanjaro*, the final reverie of a big game hunter dying of gangrene in the bush. With its savage beauty and the looming mountain, Amboseli, running in a quadrilateral shape along Kenya's border with Tanzania, is one of the most scenic of Kenya's National Parks.

Amboseli consists of swamps and bush: broken forests and stretches of plain with drier bush as an overall surround. Parts of the reserve consist of dust bowls of brilliance and beauty, scintillating mirages, and dust storms of volcanic ash thicker than an English fog. Much of the terrains consists of lava rocks thrown out by Kilimanjaro's prehistoric volcanic activity.

The reserve—Ol Tukai, 130 miles south of Nairobi, is its heart—takes its name from a large lake bed (some seven miles from the lodges and camping areas of Ol Tukai) on which there are the skeletons of giraffe and where cheetahs sometimes make a kill in a natural arena in full view of tourists. Only in seasons of heavy rain does the lake contain any significant water. In dry weather, safari vehicles drive across its checkerboard of dried mud.

At other times, the heat haze rising from the lake forms a forest mirage that recedes as the visitor approaches, making it difficult to distinguish between the illusion and the lake water.

Everywhere Mount Kilimanjaro stands out in its glistening, snow-mantled glory.

Bird-watchers rarely have a dull minute. There are snake-hunting secretary birds mincing through the grasslands with a quill-pen behind one ear; toucan-like hornbills mingle with plump guinea fowl, while along the swamps kingfishers, long-toed plovers, lilac-breasted rollers and nectar-sipping sunbirds on flickering wings add dazzling colour to the scene.

Amboseli was once the home of the most photographed wild animal alive that went under the prosaic name of 'Gertie'. She was a rhino with a heart of gold, and a fantastic 34¼'' long horn. Sadly, like the mountain gorillas of

Rwanda that have been shot by poachers for their heads to be sold as tourist 'trophies', she became too trusting of human beings – the scientists and other visitors who surrounded her regularly. One day she was speared to death by four black men who were able to approach her easily.

Rhino-poaching in Amboseli is still a grave problem, taxing the wardens and game scouts. There, as elsewhere in the country, the rhino numbers have been drastically depleted, and a Presidential Decree has been issued to protect them throughout Kenya.

The story of the Amboseli elephants, told by an attractive young American woman, Cynthia Moss, in her book *Portraits in the Wild*, is a brighter one.

Since 1972, Cynthia has been one of their unofficial guardians. From her tent near Ol Tukai, she drives out into the bush each day to study the social behaviour of the great creatures for America's African Wildlife Leadership Foundation. She now knows more than 400 Amboseli elephants by name (identified by the shape, or an ear, a scar on a leg, and so on) and most of them know and accept her.

Cynthia Moss and Drs Harvey Croze and Iain Douglas-Hamilton, with whom she worked in her early days as a researcher of elephant life styles, are among the world's leading authorities on the domestic affairs of the mightiest mammals of East Africa.

While the elephant – using its nose as a hand and with loose, wrinkled skin and huge ears – may be an object of mirth in circuses and zoos, it is loved and respected by people from all over the world. In Africa it is almost a mythical animal, the subject of countless legends.

There is something special about the elephant, says Cynthia Moss. Not just its size, its long life, its almost-human feelings or its ivory. There is something else, perhaps its intelligence, that somehow sets it apart from all other African animals.

On our way to the coast whether by road or by rail we pass through Kenya's largest National Park: Tsavo. Elephants, thousands of them are its principal attraction. Much of Tsavo's 8,000 square miles is dry, thorn-bush country, quite unsuitable for stockkeeping and so, unlike the other reserves described in this chapter, not part of Maasai country.

The Park is split by the main Nairobi-Mombasa road into Tsavo West and Tsavo East.

Tsavo West is most easily reached from Mtito Ndei – halfway to or from the sea and variously described as 'The Valley of the Eagles' and 'The Forest of Vultures', although it is little more than a collection of petrol stations – as these days a lot of people travel on the tourist circuit from Amboseli. With its riverine circuits, volcanic hills, magnificent views, typical African plains and forested mountains it has a different, perhaps more striking, ecological character than Tsavo East.

Tsavo West has fewer elephant than its sister reserve, but more cheetah and impala.

Its best viewing hill is known as 'Poachers' Lookout', and near Kiliguni Lodge is a recently extinct volcano called 'Shaitani' (Devil) that is said to have once buried a tribal village in red-hot lava. Word has it that if the visitor listens intently he will hear people talking, dogs barking, sheep bleating and cattle lowing in a ghost settlement deep under the ground.

The chief attraction, near Kiliguni, is Mzima, an oasis fed with millions of gallons of crystal-clear water each day from the green-grey, ash-and-cinder cones of the volcanic Chyulu Hills on the horizon. One of the youngest mountain-cum-hill ranges in being, the green Chyulus rise to 7,000 ft., attract a heavy rainfall and act like a sponge to feed Mzima springs from beneath a barren, blackened landscape. It is probable that eruptions occurred during the past few hundred years among the Chyulus, and that they were within the memory of tribal oral traditions. The sweet 'champagne' water they supply to Mzima is piped more than a hundred miles to Mombasa as the city's main supply.

Surrounded by squat palms and trees of heavy foliage in which vervet monkeys leap from branch to branch, the broad, deep pool of Mzima has a viewing chamber of plate-glass sunk into its bank. Through this one may see hippo sporting in ponderous underwater 'ballets', or stand in safety nose-to-nose with a crocodile.

After that experience, there's elephant-at-your-feet as you lounge on the long, open verandah of Kiliguni Lodge where a polite, whimsical notice requests guests to eat and drink quietly so as not to disturb the animals!

Kiliguni is the only lodge in Tsavo with views of both Kilimanjaro and the Chyulus. Its verandah overlooks a large waterhole and here lions — clearly related to those man-eaters of Tsavo at large at the time the railway was being constructed — have been photographed attacking elephants, a rare and dramatic sight.

The lodge claims to be one of the few places in Africa where the 'Big Five' — lion, elephant, Cape buffalo and leopard — have been seen at the same time around a floodlit waterhole.

At another lodge in the park, elephant peer in at bedroom windows.

An over-eager baby tusker there tumbled into a deep waterhole and, with heart-rending squeals, was in danger of drowning. As I watched this drama, the mother broke from the herd, snatched up the weighty youngster in her trunk and flung him to the safety of the shore . . .

Although part of the same water system from the Kilimanjaro massif, lakes Jipe and Chala in the Tsavo West area are entirely different in character.

Jipe is a sheet of alkaline water surrounded by reed swamps while Chala is a crater lake filled with clear, deep water surrounded by rocky walls. Lake Jipe has no regular outlet, but Chala has a subterranean run-off.

From the air, hippo tracks can be seen on the bed of Jipe — possibly proving the brutes prefer to walk underwater rather than swim. On the other hand, the crocodiles of Lake Chala are so aggressive they often threaten fishermen's boats.

There's a Hilton in the wilderness on the way to Tsavo East from the lakes — two Hiltons in fact. One is the Taita Hills Lodge, a departure point for both sections of Tsavo National Park. With Hilton splendour, the lodge has spacious, luxuriously-furnished bedrooms with baths, a big game hunting motif in the dining room and a circular, high-ceilinged lounge with a huge fireplace supporting a three-storey high stone chimney.

'Sundowners', Kenya parlance for cocktails, are served around the lodge's swimming pool in the late afternoon.

The other Hilton, near the Taita Hills Lodge, is the 'Salt Lick', a complex of towers roofed in African thatch and perched on top of concrete stilts with inter-connecting, bridge-like walkways. The name is taken from its setting, a natural salt pan that is a meeting place (adjacent to watering holes) for the neighbourhood's salt-hungry game. At 'Salt Lick', day and night, there are elephant and their calves, lions, giraffe, baboons and numerous species of graceful antelope. Game-viewing is from either the broad, open terrace or from a secure, specially constructed ground-level bunker — where the animals can be seen and photographed through the steel bars of a window.

Crossing the Nairobi-Mombasa highway into Tsavo East, it is possible to see pink — certainly, reddish — elephants without having had a single drink. A good deal of the earth of Tsavo East, bigger than Wales and one of Africa's largest animal preserves, is brick-red and the thousands of elephant there delight in spraying themselves with its dust or muddy waters, hence the somewhat disturbing illusion on first encounter.

Tsavo East is typical African bush country with spindly-tree scrub, odd-shaped hills and outcrops, riverine vegetation, a flat, coastal hinterland, and tracts where grassland has triumphed after a bush-fire or where trees have been destroyed by browsing elephant. Each fully-grown elephant can eat from 400 to 600 lb. of grasses, bark, leaves, branches, fruit and seed pods a day, and drink up to 50 gallons of water in the same period. They will knock over a tree just to get at a few juicy top leaves. They will bore into, and destroy, (when much of Tsavo East looks like a Great War battlefield) baobab trees for water in times of severe drought. They will dig deep holes in the beds of dried-up rivers, scraping away the sand with their forelegs and deepening the 'well' with their trunks and tusks. The babies queue up behind their elders for a drink.

The railway line, as well as the main road alongside, forms one boundary of Tsavo East. Elephant grazing on the grass verges will lumber back across the tracks into the safety of the park if they feel threatened by human predators.

The northern region of the park is hot and waterless.

Attracted by glittering brass shoulder badges, ostriches line up behind game scouts on parade with their rifles outside the park headquarters near Voi. Here were raised 'The Orphans of Tsavo', young elephants and rhinos, guarded by an African keeper under a black umbrella, who had been rescued and reared by the warden and his wife after their parents had been slaughtered by poachers.

The 'Big Five' can be found in Tsavo East's trackless bush, and from atop a whale-shaped outcrop called Mudanda Rock one can sit in perfect safety and comfort watching the elephants wallowing and drinking in a natural dam below formed by runoff rainwater from the rock.

The Voi Safari Lodge in Tsavo East built on living rock, features cocktails like 'Green Mamba', 'Lion's Whisker' and 'Tsavo Sunset', and is a good vantage point from which to spot the Lesser kudu, a reduced copy of its big brother the Greater kudu.

The Lesser kudu, a markedly handsome animal with a 'rocking horse' gallop, likes the semi-arid, thorn-bush country of Tsavo and can be seen early morning or evening in small herds feeding on seedpods, leaves and wild fruits. The rams have a silky-grey coat with a dozen white vertical stripes, white bars on the throat and lower neck and horns growing in three spirals. The ewes are hornless, but have white-fringed ears and are equally graceful and striking in appearance.

Another feature of Tsavo East is one of the greatest flows of lava known to man, the 200-mile long Yatta plateau. A narrow flat-topped ridge, it stretches from Ol Doinyo Sabuk Mountain in southern Kenya to Sobo in Tsavo East. The edge of the plateau is formed by a significant cliff-line that is clearly visible from the main Nairobi-Mombasa road.

MOUNT KILIMANJARO

Above: Crater rim seen from Gilman's Point

Below: Ice cliffs around the crater rim at about 18,000 ft

Right: View of Mount Kilimanjaro from the Amboseli Plain –
maned lion in the foreground

Maasai herdsboy

Maasai elder and moran

Maasai cattle in a gorge near Olorgasailie, Rift Valley

Maasai women

Balloon safari over Keekerok, Maasai Mara

Lion in the Maasai Mara

Siesta!

Lioness and cubs on buffalo kill

Above left: Wild dog
Above right: Black-backed jackal
Below: Ruppell's Griffon vultures on buffalo carcass (lion kill)

Burchell's zebra with calf

Rhino with red-billed oxpeckers

Far left: Young impalas
Left: Dik-dik
Right: Ross's turaco
Far left below: Maasai giraffe
Left below: Coke's hartebeest
Below: Red-billed hornbill

Flamingo and wildebeest, Lake Magadi

Above: Acacia brevispica, Maasai Mara
Below: Crinum kirkii, Loita Hills

Mara River

Group of elephants

Baobab showing characteristic elephant damage

Elephant dusting

LAKE JIPE

Left: Purple heron on
    a reed island
Below: Spoonbills
Right: White pelican

Taita Hills

Group of zebras –
Chyulu Hills in the background

Acacia with Weaver birds nests, Tsavo East

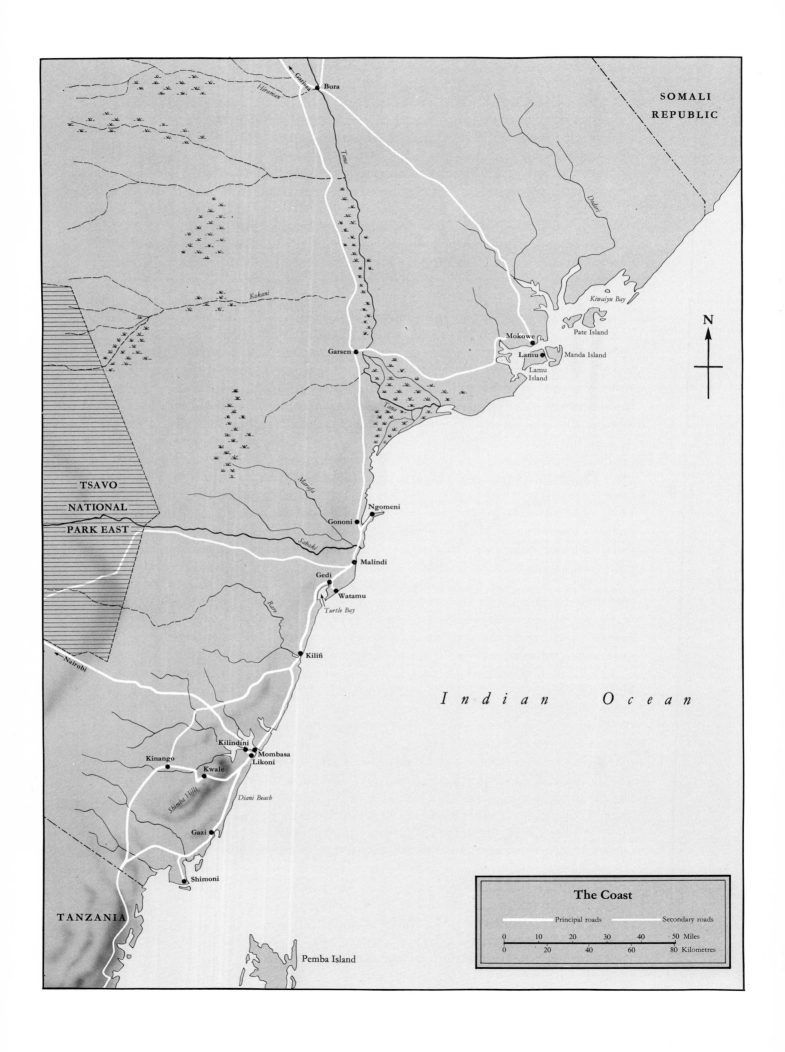

SOMALI
REPUBLIC

Daduri

Hiraman

Garissa
Bura

Tana

Kokani

Kiwaiyu Bay

N

Mokowe
Pate Island
Garsen
Lamu
Manda Island
Lamu
Island

Tana

Marafa

Ngomeni
TSAVO
Gononi
Sabaki
NATIONAL
Malindi

PARK EAST
Gedi
Watamu
Turtle Bay

Rare

Indian Ocean

Kilifi

Nairobi

Kilindini
Kinango
Mombasa
Kwale
Likoni
Shimba Hills
Diani Beach

Gazi

Shimoni

TANZANIA

The Coast

Principal roads   Secondary roads

0   10   20   30   40   50 Miles

0   20   40   60   80 Kilometres

Pemba Island

6

The Enchanted Coast

When the tourist feels he or she needs a change from the excitement of watching Africa's wild beasts in their natural habitats, the Kenya coast — sometimes called 'The Coral Coast' — offers the relaxations of aquamarine lagoons and silvery, unpolluted shores, marine national parks teeming with vividly-patterned fish, sailing in a 32 ft. yacht or an African fisherman's crude outrigger, goggling and scuba-diving or just acquiring a mahogany tan under a palm tree.

'Paradise in the sun' . . . 'One of the world's finest holiday areas' . . . 'A tropical Shangri-La' . . . The clichés of tourism have been increasingly applied over the years to Kenya's Indian Ocean coast. Hotels, curio shops, beach boutiques, night clubs and other enterprises catering solely to visitors have been multiplying. Yet it should still be a long time before the beauty and character of the Coral Coast is tarnished. The more tasteful and imaginative hotels, restaurants of high international standards and well-run deep-sea fishing clubs enhance the delights of a scintillating sea.

African life, transformed by history here and there into an Arab style, impinges on the white man and his water sports in the ever-growing resorts. For instance, superstition and belief in magic are strong along this enchanted coast. 'Anti-witchcraft medicine' advertises a neatly-painted board beside a tarred road much travelled by tourists.

The entire history of the coast has been one of adapting to strange visitors and intruders— Arab, Portuguese, Indian or British. Mixing and melding is an old coastal custom.

Islands, uncrowded beaches, historic towns, old ports, day-long sunshine, fascinating local cultures and a tranquil sea are the principal delights for visitors, both those from abroad and up-country. Meanwhile everyday life goes on around the vacation spots for the Giriama tribespeople (their women topless, the men in 'skirts' of brightly-patterned cloth), the Bajun fishermen of the north and the Mijikenda in the south. Growing bananas, coconuts, maize or sisal; line-fishing in dug-out canoes; offering their limes, pineapples and paw-paw in the markets; walking the roads or working in their villages, the indigenous people smilingly tolerate the latest invaders on their historic and lovely shores.

Visited in turn by Arab dhows, Portugese galleons, British merchantmen and modern luxury liners, Mombasa owes its status as one of the biggest and most important ports of the Indian Ocean to a *mlango*, or 'door', in a reef that stretches the 300-mile length of the Kenya coastline.

The rambling island city's hallmarks are two sets of mammoth elephant tusks, painted ivory on sheet metal, that tower over a dual carriageway leading from the heart of the city to the modern harbour of Kilindini, or 'Place of Deep Water'.

Having been the centre of ancient power struggles to rule the coast and the reservoir of slaves and ivory in the interior, Mombasa was originally named 'The Island of War'.

The Old Town is a maze of narrow streets (in one only *khangas*, wrap-around cloths of a hundred tints and patterns, are sold); Brahmin temples; phallic minarets; raucous, crowded fish-markets; Persian carpets; stout ornamental doors with sharp brass studs (that once kept elephants from rubbing their backsides on the wood): women descendants of slavers' wives dressed from head to toes in swirling, black *bui buis*, and flamboyant flame trees.

The site of Mombasa's Holy Ghost Cathedral was bought in 1891 by a priest who arrived in the town disguised as an Arab trader.

The central railway station has a section for 'Upper Classes Only', and one of Mombasa's plethora of drab hole-in-corner 'hotels' advertises 'Common and attached baths'.

Another city sign — at the changing rooms by the swimming pool of the staid Mombasa Club — exhorts bathers to leave their money and valuables with the receptionist for safe keeping — 'At your own risk'.

Mombasa is the principal port of Kenya, and also handles most of land-locked Uganda's imports and exports. Along the flowered seafront, named Mama Ngina Drive after Kenyatta's widow, are huge baobab trees with stout girths and root-like branches — the Africans say God planted them upside down — that turn coppery at sunset.

Mombasa is an ideal centre from which to explore the coastline, south to the Tanzanian border and north to the islands of Lamu.

The crossing to the southern part of the mainland is made at Likoni by large, motorised ferries that take buses, lorries, cars, cyclists, donkey carts and foot passengers. The first Likoni ferries were two rowing boats, towing cattle tied astern.

The southern road runs through large coconut and sugar plantations, interspersed with drowsy villages of coral-stone and reed-thatch homes.

Seaward is the magnificent Diani beach, six miles of white sand that rivals Bondi and Hawaii, bordered by feathery casuarinas and palm-groves sighing in the breeze. Gardens of scarlet poinsettia, bougainvillaea, evergreen oleanders and waxen gardenias complete the idyllic scene.

Near the Trade Winds Hotel on Diani is a 500-year-old baobab, protected from the axe by presidential decree. Its trunk is 72 ft. in circumference.

Off the coastal road, past a house that was the torture chamber in the 1840's of a Mazrui 'shaikh', who suffocated those of his victims who survived red-hot irons and racks, in the fumes of roasting chillis, is a unique little game park, the Shimba Hills.

How many other nature reserves he may have visited, it is unlikely the visitor will have seen the Shimba Hills' most distinguished inmate, the rare roan antelope. By virtue of its size (nearly as big as the easily-domesticated eland) and perfect proportions, the roan, with a wiry coat of rufous-grey, short, ridged horns and tuft-tipped, donkey-like ears, is considered to be one of the finest of African antelopes.

It was in danger of extinction in Kenya at the hands of poachers. A few

174

years ago one of the last remaining herds was rounded up by horsemen and helicopters on an up-country ranch and translocated to the Shimba Hills Reserve. They are now breeding slowly in company with the handsome and dignified sable antelope with its long, swept-back horns that keep the big cats at bay.

The game park, covering 74 square miles, is open country with tracts of bush and forest, and hilltop views of the sea. The flora includes trees whose fruit is coveted by the Shimba elephants. At certain times of the year they can be seen lurching, squint-eyed, from tree to tree. The plum-like fruit ferments in the elephants' stomachs; then the more they drink at the waterholes, the drunker they get.

Towards the end of the southern section of the coastal road there is Gazi with its 1,000-acre coconut estate, and a turn-off to Shimoni, Swahili for 'The Place of the Hole'. Slaves were hidden in the village's bat-ridden caves before being shipped aboard blockade-running dhows. Now Shimoni is the site of the well-known Pemba Channel Fishing Club with a fleet of fast, marlin-hunting craft equipped with ship-to-shore radios and whippy outriggers.

The fish of the Coral Coast are as fascinating and varied as the wild animals of the land. Way out in the inky-black waters beyond the 100-fathom line of the Indian Ocean lurk the 1,000 lb. striped or black marlin, the dream of every big game fisherman. There too, is the sleek sailfish, electric-blue spots on its shining, dark body, that leaps clear of the waves and dances on a crescent tail when hooked.

As in the bush, where he looks for vultures circling over a lion kill, the sportsman watches the birds for signs of a possible fishing trophy. Terns diving into the sea after fluttering over the waves are a signal to make a dash to the spot in the boat. The birds are snatching up small fish whose shoals are preyed upon by larger species and those, in turn, by the big-fin predators.

Closer to the shore is the torpedo-bodied bonito, a relative of the tunny, that shoots from the deep to grab a flying fish in mid-air. There is often a race for the prize with the swift dolphin-fish or *felusi*, not to be confused with true dolphins which are mammals. The *felusi* grows to lengths of up to six feet and probably got its Western name from the fact that, like a dolphin or porpoise, it can leap high out of the water. The Giriama and Bajun outrigger fishermen of the coast have written poems of praise in Swahili to this fish of glorious colouring — bluish-black with golden tints on silver and a yellowish belly with blue spots; all with flashes of green, blue and pink when landed and dying at the bottom of the fisherman's canoe.

The seaward sides of the coral reefs are the haunts of a fish more dangerous and aggressive than a shark — the man-sized, crocodile-jawed barracuda, tiger of the sea, that can cripple a swimmer with one bite.

Equally fearsome are the ten-foot-long moray eels lurking in the coral caverns where 800 lb. groupers, or rock cod, wait for the unwary fish to swim into gaping jaws.

Out there also are the dugongs or sea cows that, despite their slug-like ugliness, gave rise to the mariners' tales of mermaids.

The best marine shows are in the shoreward lagoons behind the coral reefs, themselves consisting of myraids of miniscule, predatory beings (living on top of ramparts of dead coral) that are phosphorescent and glow in the light of the moon.

In the translucent 'underwater zoos' of Kenya's three marine national parks, at Shimoni, Malindi and Watamu, the first of their kind in Africa, there are short fish, long fish, flat fish, and fat fish, that provide riots of colour.

Here you can swim with a turtle.

The scorpion fish with fronds of fins like a peacock's tail blends perfectly with the coral beds, seaweed and other tropical fishes, but is as poisonous as it is fascinating and attractive.

There is the jaunty, pinkish-red 'Johnny' with yellow streaks; jet-black sea bream, a delicacy grilled over charcoal, and the purple wrasse with 'windows' on its flanks. The females make nests of seaweed for their eggs.

Part of the gaudy company are zebra fish, tiger-striped eels and starfish looking as though they had been dipped in crimson house-paint.

Even the living coral is preyed upon by fish like the yellow, black and white moon butterflyfish that has a pointed mouth for getting into crevices and looks like Piglet. Its companions are the orange-and-gold sea perch; the flame-red squirrelfish, larger than the household goldfish; the obese, white-and-blue striped emperor angelfish; the yellow and Cambridge-blue angelfish; the aptly-named clown-fish and the white-spotted pufferfish with scales resembling a leopard's coat.

There is an octopus motionless in a rock cave, surrounded by shoals of inquisitive squids and cuttlefish which emit a black smokescreen when alarmed by the onset of a silver-grey shark that could have slipped through a gap in the reef. Spiny lobsters weave among colonies of transparent prawns; and a species of sea urchin that has no eyes directs its spines by 'radar' at an intruder.

There are shells of every shape and colour in and around the marine parks but it is an offence to collect them, or to catch any fish.

Along the shore there are bustling bubbler crabs that feed on the sea fluid squeezed from pellets of sand. And here is the remarkable mud skipper that begins life as a normal fish but spends much of its later years hopping across the sand and mud flats in search of insects, breathing through a vascular tail dangling in the water. Its strange skill also enables it to seek cooler pools inside the reef when the tide has receded and its own water gets too hot under a fierce sun.

Out of Mombasa, the road to the north was reached until recently over a 50-year-old pontoon bridge with a toll of a shilling a car. The fee had remained unchanged from way back, despite galloping inflation.

The Japanese have now built a new bridge.

At the start of the journey north, overlooking Mombasa's old harbour, is one of the best restaurants in Africa — an elegant Moorish-style structure where dinner of bisque, grilled lobster and a mango sorbet on the terrace under the stars is an *Arabian Nights* delight.

From here to the Lamu archipelago is one long playground, rivalling the south with a host of hotels offering every kind of water sport; sun, sea and sand in generous measures; disco dancing and barbecues beneath a theatrical, buttermilk moon.

Kilifi, halfway between Mombasa and Malindi, has pleasant anchorages for yachts and the boats of big game fishermen, as well as being a haunt of water-skiers.

It has a new and thriving cashew nut industry, surrounded by the cashew trees of dark green foliage. The nut hangs from a strawberry-coloured 'fruit' that gives off a sickly scent, and its juice is tart and astringent. While the nut, plain or roasted, is generally found among cocktail snacks, the cashew-shell mush obtained from grinding is used in brake linings.

Kilifi stands at the mouth of a wide creek where fine prawns are netted, and carmine bee-eaters fly home at dusk to their mangrove swamps like flashes of flame in the dying sun.

After the Kilifi ferry, the road runs through a natural ebony forest in which are hidden the Zanzibar duiker, a small antelope, and the Sokoke pipit.

Two brief diversions before Malindi provide vivid contrasts.

The eerie ruins of Gedi, lying under a pall of deep silence in a forest where the trees are festooned with snakes, consist of a surrounding wall, a palace, large and small mosques, a market, three pillar tombs and many crumbling mansions. The headlights of motorists daring to visit the ghost city at night have been known to fail suddenly, and Gedi has its own *djinn* that, attracted by a scrawled spell, was supposed to have lived in a tall clay pot as a sort of watchdog to attack and scare off ill-intentioned visitors. It seems to have lost its power around 1650.

Close to the enigma of Gedi are 'swinging' Watamu and Turtle Bay (named after the sea-eroded tortoise shaped banks of coral) where each week there are intakes of hundreds of holidaymakers from West Germany responding to lurid advertisements in their newspapers and magazines. The men are promised compliant, dusky maidens and every woman a black Adonis. Reality is more sordid — mushroom 'day and night' drinking clubs frequented by African gigolos in natty striped bathing trunks (who permanently need a £10 loan to bring their sister from Uganda to attend Nairobi University), and tribal dancing girls with voluptuous, but straw-padded, bottoms and grubby brassieres.

Malindi too has become a 'Little Germany' of Teutonic package tours, a far cry from Milton's 'Melind' and the 13th century geographer who wrote of 'tiger hunts' there. But morals may have improved a little since the days of a Chinese chronicler who claimed that the people of 'Ma-Lin' were 'black, fierce . . . and not ashamed of debauching the wives of their fathers'.

After the Second World War, Malindi acquired a split personality. On one side, the town (where signs in German now abound) was filled with Giriama peasant farmers, fishermen who brought their catches ashore from lateen-sailed *ngalawas* to be auctioned off by a Hollywood Arab with a blackthorn stick, and palm-toddy runners who arrived in relays with off-white 'wine' (drawn from the trunks of palm trees) in plastic containers lashed to the carrier racks of their bicycles.* On the other hand, Malindi became an 'in' place for tourism: and the aged wealthy, or the merely rich, built gracious homes that faced placid lagoons and had large grounds with hibiscus and frangipani set among the lawns.

Up to fifty percent of the town's jobs are now in the tourist or big game fishing industries — waiters, safari guides, and coxwains of the boats that speed seaward for ten or fifteen miles in search of marlin, barracuda, shark, sailfish, kingfish, the swift wahoo or the five-fingered jack that has God's finger and thumb prints near its gills. Big fish caught off the Kenya coast have broken several world records.

Ernest Hemingway, that deep-sea fishing expert, followed the sport out of Malindi — where he also did a little writing and his share of drinking, at a local hotel. When visiting literati ask to see his room or the stool at the bar on which

---

* The trade still goes on.

he might have sat, the black receptionist is apt to ask with genuine bewilderment 'Ernest who?'

Malindi is the one seaside resort that has a truly golden beach. It glitters or 'glisters' in the noonday sun. The 'gold', sadly, is coastal schist mixed in with the sand and, like the Sabaki River silt that at flood times turns the sea dark red, is the bane of bathers.

A local herpetologist runs snake-catching safaris from Malindi, and even gets enough enthusiasts with forked sticks to make up small parties.

Not all of Kenya's coast is tied to the past. In a wide bay, three miles off Ngomeni, a fishing village just north of Malindi, stands a wide platform for launching space rockets – called San Marco – and a control platform, Santa Rita. There teams of Italian and American space scientists and technicians find the equatorial haze of the heavens conducive to space research. Whenever a rocket is launched the African fishermen and their families gather on shore to cheer and marvel at the fiery-tailed phenomenon. One of the San Marco satellites provided the first indirect evidence of the existence of 'black holes' in the universe.

Within sight of the San Marco project and its 'blazing snakes', it is possible to spend a day like a Crusoe castaway and forget the strains and stresses of modern civilisation.

A Bajun* 'gondolier', chanting in Swahili the charms of any woman passenger, poles a flat-bottom boat across a shallow channel to Robinson Island. The central point is a rough shelter of mangrove poles, palm fronds and canvas facing the sea. There are cane divans on which to recover from an excellent, moderately-priced meal of braised coconut chips, fresh-boiled crab (with cudgels to smash the claws on the rough wooden table), palm salad, fried cod, or an Arab-Swahili curry called *mango massala*. These island dishes are followed by a slice of Malindi melon and Arab coffee poured from conical brass pots from the clove island of Zanzibar, and laced with pressed coconut cream.

The smiling young waiters and waitresses are as informally, and scantily, dressed as the lotus-eating guests.

Grilled young barracuda, served with gin and the milk of a green coconut (the drink is called *madafu*), is a delicacy of the Kenya coast, along with mangrove oysters baked in their shells (with garlic and bread crumbs) over a driftwood fire on the beach. In most of the country's hotels and safari lodges, the meals prepared by European-trained black chefs are of excellent standard. Also on offer throughout the land are such tasty traditional African meals as *ugali*, the Kikuyu stew of lamb, wild spinach and boiled maize; *kuku* (chicken) broiled with green bananas which is a feast for the Kamba (who are noted woodcarvers), or succulent slices of grilled bush-pig served with boiled sweet potatoes.

Beyond Robinson Island to Lamu the rutted road is generally closed in the heavy wet season of April and May, but there is an air charter service from Malindi to Lamu that takes only half-an-hour. The plane flies over a wide, beautiful bay that Vasco da Gama named 'Formosa'– he thought it was the first one in India– and the valley of the Tana, Kenya's largest river where the Galla people sport brilliant blue clothes like the sea, river and lakes around them and Orma girls proudly display their intricate bracelets and necklaces.

Walk backwards in time for a few hundred years and you are in Lamu town,

---

* Inhabitant of the Lamu Islands.

lyrically described by a Nairobi University professor as 'one of the most restful places on earth'.

Lamu is a living museum, typical of the romantic population centres that once existed along the East African coast. As such, it is Kenya's Kathmandu, attracting hippies, archaeologists and staid, elderly tourists alike.

Cars and bicycles are banned. Every few steps through the town's cramped streets with their ornate, overhanging balconies give glimpses of a calm, barely changing, way of life: dim, cool stores selling hand-woven carpets; low-ceilinged coffee-shops; goldsmiths, woodcarvers, tailors, and silversmiths sit bent over their delicate work, and dhow chandlers scurry to and fro, past stalls piled high with mangoes that have skins like sundown.

There are copper trays the size of cartwheels for sale, and jewelled Arab daggers and ebony thrones inlaid with ivory.

Amid the maze of twisting, narrow streets stands a white, towered fort with a single black cannon that was once a sultan's palace. It is now the town prison.

As little as a dozen years ago, Lamu had no electricity. It still has no advertisement hoardings, and the − open air − cinema is a sheet stretched between two palms. *Ben Hur* was the last big attraction.

'It is refreshing to find one place in the world that does not pretend to believe in progress', wrote James Kirkman, an archaeologist who worked for several years in the Lamu group of islands.

Lamu was once a trading town bolstered by slavery, like Mombasa and Malindi, but it collapsed economically in 1900. The skin colours of its peoples vary from black to sepia, revealing a great diversity of racial origins. The large majority of Lamu folk, however, are orthodox Moslems, the men wearing the flowing white *khanzu* and the women swathed in purdah black (but with no veil, as a gesture to modernity).

The inhabitants chew a mildly narcotic combination of betel nut, tobacco, powdered limes and the heart-leaf of the *tambuu* vine.

Their principal religious festival is the *maulidi* when they spend an entire week feasting, chanting and dancing — with Catherine wheels of pastel hues in the main square — in celebration of the Prophet's birthday.

Lithe Somali cattle-drivers mingle in streets barely wide enough for man or donkey. White-gowned Lamu elders bow to kiss the hand of a passing *shariff*; and the only insistent communications are the *muezzins'* calls to prayer from the island's thirty or so mosques.

The strong, extensive sea wall, guarded by rusting cannons, is reached past coral-stone houses with shuttered windows and cool courtyards where fountains play among bowers of sweet-scented moonflowers. White men have restored much of Lamu's 18th-century architecture.

Mangrove poles bartered for salt and carpets are loaded aboard dhows moored off the wall by relays of perspiring African stevedores, wearing only ragged shorts or a length of cloth. Tough Lamu *boriti* — the poles hacked from the mangrove swamps around the island — is prized in Arabia for building purposes as it is resistant to white ants.

Lamu's coastal dhows, the smaller *jahazis*, on which the town depends for a good deal of its supplies, stage races (hardly Blue Riband, but exciting enough) now and then between Mombasa, and their home town.

There is a story, at least half true, concerning two captains who had made an equal number of victory voyages from Mombasa and were now to stage a final race to decide which one was 'The Greyhound of the Seas', or something similar. One skipper sneaked off to a witchdoctor who gave him a magic potion to scatter in the path of his rival to bring him misfortune. This having been done during the race, the mast of the *nakhoda* (captain) overhauling him duly snapped and — one assumes with a devilish laugh — the villain sailed on to Lamu.

But wait — the coastal people, that mixture of Arabs and Africans, are no fools. The captain of the crippled dhow had also been to a witchdoctor, for an even more powerful potion of ground-up baboon bones and snakes' eyes guaranteed to overcome all misfortunes when scattered round the deck.

Sure enough, with the broken mast quickly repaired by the crew and the voodoo powder strewn about, the dhow forged ahead 'like a lion' and, to welcoming blasts on a great *siwa* horn of silver and ivory, zoomed past the other vessel at the entrance to Lamu channel.

Both men, we are told, have now retired from the sea and are helping to build *jahazis* with wooden rivets and fish-oil 'varnish' on the mud flats beyond the town.

Lamu has its own idiosyncratic charm.

Queen Victoria's first vice-consul there was Rider Haggard's brother, Jack. At one time Lamu had a naked beachcomber, and one man lived alone in a house there for forty years. Another wild character named Petley was reputed to have strangled leopards bare-handed, and is said to haunt the pagoda-style inn he put up on the Lamu waterfront. Here he would knock down any guest he disliked or who had the temerity to complain about the less-than-three-star food and accommodation.

The coinage is another curiosity of the Lamu group. Still circulating among the islands is the Austrian Maria Theresia dollar, once legal tender, and a few small US gold coins said to have been distributed to the natives in 1875 by the American newsman-explorer who found Dr Livingstone, Henry Morton Stanley. (They are traditionally worn by the Bajun as a nose-piece.)

In this closing chapter it is perhaps fitting to turn back a few more pages of history and sail north of Lamu town, past small, black islands that are but clumps of mangroves in shallow water. Our dhow heels steeply to the monsoon under a swollen sail of patched canvas.

The island of Manda opposite Lamu is the oldest known site on the Kenya coast. Its autocratic peoples told the Portuguese invaders in 1589 that only the sun and moon could get into their town. They were wrong. So too were the islanders from up-coast who were confident they could conquer Lamu island's first Arab settlement, the 7th-century town of Hidabu overlooking the ocean.

On Pate, a state founded on a northern island in the 14th century and a one-time rival to Mombasa, the sultan's palace is but a heap of rubble buried beneath the sand.

Thirty miles from the Somali border is the desert island village of Kiwaiyu. Elephants coming in from the hinterlands to cool off in the sea lumber across the beach near a well-appointed tented camp set up for surfing enthusiasts, and plain sunworshippers, from Europe. Crab cooked in coconut oil and ginger is the local speciality.

Further north, at Ishakani, are some of the best preserved ruins in East Africa. Historian Jim de Vere Allen, a Kenyan citizen, believes they are the remains of an ancient coastal culture known as 'Swahilini'. Buried in the matted bush ashore are huge tombs of coral-stone, ruined houses and places of worship of no known Arab origin. The tombs bear large, embossed designs more like a variety of brands of a cattle-owning tribespeople than anything of Islamic origin, according to Allen.

Was the Lamu archipelago once the heart of an African civilisation that has long since passed into oblivion?

Such is the question mark that hangs over the windswept dunes of that lonely Kenyan shore where yet another of mankind's riddles lies waiting to be solved.

In the old quarters of Mombasa

Aerial view of Mombasa

Giriama in their *ngalawas*

Delamere Cup Fishing Competition
at Mnarani Club

Giriama children carrying water gourds

Pokoma and cattle by the Tana River near Garsen

Carmen bee-eaters in an acacia, Boni forest

Butterflies mating (*Acraea natalica*)

The ruins of Gedi

Sable antelope, Shimba Hills

Sykes monkey, Gedi forest

Giriama fishermen pulling in their sardine catch, Diani Beach

Turtle Bay, Watamu

Jahazi off Lamu

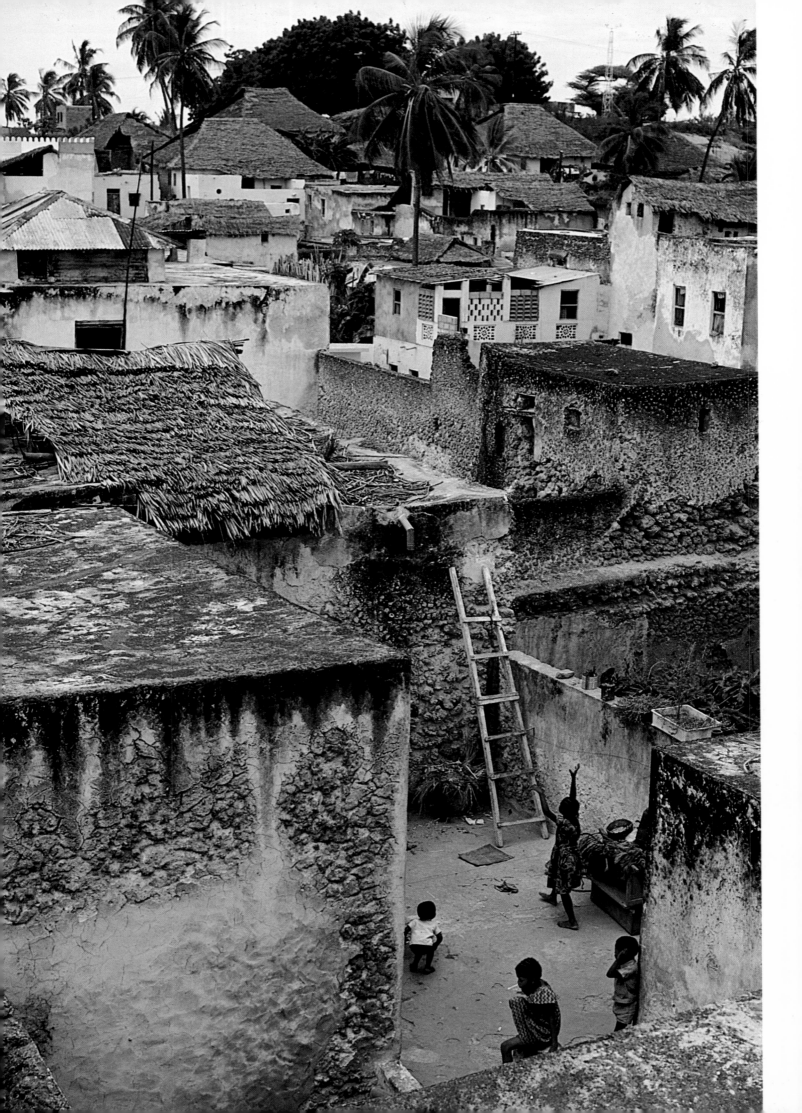

Rooftop view of the old town of Lamu

Shela Mosque – with Manda Island in the background

Swahili girl in *bui bui*

Group of women watching Maulidi celebrations from a rooftop

Swahili women watching Habib Salih procession

Goma cane dancers during Maulidi celebrations

LAMU

Carved doorway

Detail of old door carvings

Door carvings and padlock chain

Alcove in an 18th-century house

Bougainvillaea in the patio

Rooftop of Riyadha Mosque

Earrings (*mabambo*)

Gold earplugs (*kutha*)

Herizi silver talisman

Bajun woman wearing traditional nose-ring with an 1853 California gold dollar attached

Two Lamu residents, in *kikoi* and *kofia*, enjoy a chat

BIBLIOGRAPHY

Africa Year Book, East Africa Journal, Nairobi

ADAMSON, George: *Bwana Game,* Collins and Harvill Press, London, 1968

ADAMSON, Joy: *Born Free,* Collins and Harvill Press, London, 1960

BLIXEN, Karen: *Out of Africa,* Putnam & Co. Ltd, London, 1937

BOLTON, Kenneth: *Harambee Country,* Geoffrey Bles Ltd, London, 1970

CHURCHILL, Winston S.: *My African Journey,* Hodder & Stoughton Ltd, London, 1908

FELLOWS, Lawrence: *East Africa,* Collier Macmillan Ltd, London, 1972

HEMINGWAY, Ernest: *The Green Hills of Africa,* Jonathan Cape, London, 1936. *The Snows of Kilimanjaro,* Jonathan Cape, London, 1939

HEMSING, Jan: *Old Nairobi,* Church, Orr & Associates, Nairobi, 1978

HORROBIN, Prof. David F.: *A Guide to Kenya,* East African Publishing House Ltd, Nairobi, 1975

HUXLEY, Elspeth: *The Flame Trees of Thika,* Chatto & Windus, Ltd, London, 1959

KENYATTA, Jomo: *Facing Mount Kenya,* Secker & Warburg Ltd, London, 1961

MABERLY, C. T. Astley: *Animals of East Africa,* Hodder & Stoughton Ltd, London, 1972

MAGARY, Alan & Kersten Fraser: *East Africa,* Harper & Row, New York, 1975

MOSS, Cynthia: *Portraits in the Wild,* Hamish Hamilton Ltd, London, 1976

RUARK, Robert: *Something of Value,* Hamish Hamilton Ltd, London, 1955

SNYDER, Phil: *Mount Kenya National Park,* Kenya Government, Nairobi, 1979

TOMPKINSON, Michael: *Kenya,* Ernest Benn Ltd, London, 1973

WILLIAMS, J. G.: *The Birds of East and Central Africa,* William Collins Sons & Co. Ltd, London, 1963